Lakeland
Steamers

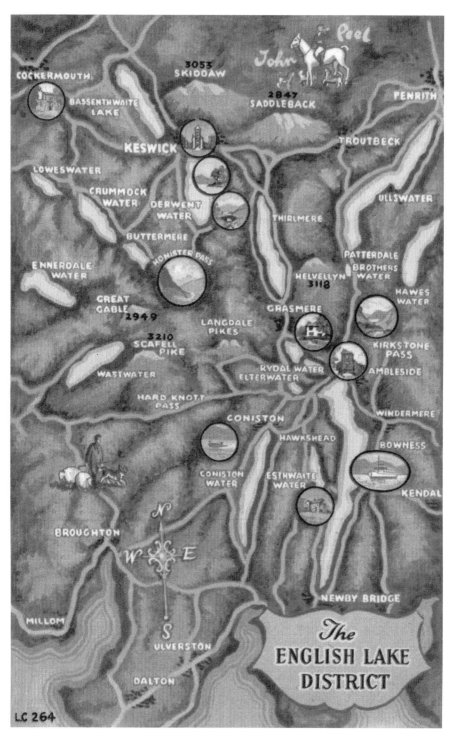

The English Lake District has been a haven for sightseeing and enjoyment since Victorian times. One of the best ways to view the varied and breathtaking Lakeland scenery is aboard a traditional lake pleasure steamer.

Lakeland
Steamers

ANDREW GLADWELL

AMBERLEY

Lake Windermere, Bowness, Westmorland.   15679.

The three most popular lakes are Windermere, Ullswater and Coniston. They are the main homes of the wonderfully stylish and nostalgic Lake District steamers. The pleasure steamers offer us a wonderful opportunity to experience transport of a bygone age and are the perfect way to view and admire the breathtaking scenery of the English Lake District. (*J & C McCutcheon Collection*)

First published 2011

Amberley Publishing
The Hill, Stroud
Gloucestershire GL5 4ER

www.amberleybooks.com

British Library Cataloguing in Publication Data.
A catalogue record for this book is available from the British Library.

ISBN 978 1 4456 0029 1

Typesetting and Origination by Amberley Publishing.
Printed in Great Britain.

Contents

Acknowledgements

This book has been written to evoke the heritage and atmosphere of the famous and well-loved steamers of the English Lake District. When compiling such a book, it's impossible to include every vessel due to the constraints of material and space. This book is therefore a taster to give a flavour of the lake transport loved by generations of visitors. In compiling this book I have been grateful for the help and co-operation of several individuals. In particular, I would like to thank Campbell McCutcheon for allowing me to use some of his wonderful material and for providing such splendid support. Thanks also to Sue Steinberg. I'm also indebted to Sabine Skae at the Dock Museum at Barrow-in-Furness for allowing me to use the stunning photographic material showing the construction of the *Swan* and *Teal* at Barrow. Their extensive archive can be viewed at www.dockmuseum.co.uk.

Websites

For details of steamer cruises on Ullswater
www.ullswater-steamers.co.uk

For details of cruises on Lake Windermere
www.windermere-lakecruises.co.uk

For cruises on Coniston's Gondola
www.nationaltrust.org.uk/main/w-gondola

Details on Coniston lake cruises
www.conistonlaunch.co.uk

Details on Derwent Water cruises
www.keswick-launch.co.uk

For further information on paddle and pleasure steamers
www.heritagesteamers.co.uk

For photographs showing ships built by Vickers of Barrow
www.dockmuseum.org.uk

For more books by the author of this book
www.andrewgladwell.co.uk

Introduction

The English Lake District has been one of the most popular of all British holiday destinations since it was first explored by tourists in the early nineteenth century. From quite modest beginnings, the tourist industry exploded in the mid-Victorian era from where it has never looked back.

The prime reason for tourism has always been the lakes themselves and there's no finer way of exploring and admiring them than on a traditional Lake District pleasure steamer. It was the railways that helped to open up the lakes for pleasure steamers. At the time there were no decent roads and travelling within the Lake District was very difficult and uncomfortable. The three main lakes of Windermere, Ullswater and Coniston therefore soon introduced lake steamers.

The use of these lakes by water craft was, of course, not new. In earlier times, boats and ferries were operated by oar or sail, but the coming of the railways bought the efficiency, grace, beauty and power of Victorian steam to the lakes. From the mid-nineteenth century onwards, once rail links had been built, a fleet of handsome steam-powered boats were introduced with names such as *Lady of the Lake*, *Swan*, *Raven*, *Tern*, *Gondola* and *Cygnet*. The remarkable fact about these steamers is that many had long careers and some have survived to this day. Now, around a century and a half later, tourists of the twenty-first century are still able to capture the ambience of the era when the Lake District was first becoming a holiday destination.

Out of the twenty major lakes in the Lake District, two in particular have always been the centre for the steamers – Windermere and Ullswater. Ullswater – the 'Lake Lucerne of England', with its breathtaking views of Helvellyn – has the very special accolade of having the oldest operational lake steamer in the UK – the *Lady of the Lake*. Such a distinction allows us to close our eyes and to experience what the Victorians enjoyed some 130 years earlier. Windermere, on the other hand, has the largest steamer fleet of any UK lake. It has remained the centre of the Lake District since the area first found prominence. The Windermere steamer fleet today includes the *Swan* and *Teal* – two large comfortable steamers built in the confident 1930s. It also includes a survivor of the Victorian era – the *Tern* of 1891. They give us a flavour, along with the fine buildings and piers that serve them, of the heyday of Lakeland steamer services; both of its Victorian and Edwardian heritage and the time of great expansion during the LMS years of the 1930s.

Other areas of the Lake District have had steamer services although not as developed as that of Windermere and Ullswater. Coniston Water has for example housed many steamers, especially those of the Furness Railway fleet, and today plays host to the extravagant and atmospheric *Gondola*, allowing passengers of the twenty-first century the opportunity of travelling back in time aboard a most special vessel. Unique and stylish steam yachts have also been popular with steamers such as *Esperance*, *Branksome* and *Dolly*, conjuring up the typical Lakeland atmosphere of *Swallows and Amazons* and Edwardian folk taking afternoon tea on the lake.

Changes in ownership have been a feature of the steamer scene since the 1850s. Perhaps one operator stands out among the others – that of the Furness Railway. The Furness Railway bought mass tourism to the Lakes in the years before the First World War. Their large and distinctive fleet of lake steamers, combined with good railway connections and talent for marketing, encouraged a huge influx of visitors. Many of these tourists came from the bustling resorts of Blackpool and Fleetwood to Barrow and onwards to the Lakes to experience the area's great charm. The *Tern* and *Gondola* are the twenty-first century legacy of the Furness Railway years.

The Lake District steamers have suffered relatively little from changes in tourism and transport needs. The 1930s expansion produced vessels that have survived to this day. Perhaps the reason why the steamers have survived is that they adapted to the changing needs of their passengers. Steam has given way to diesel power and passenger accommodation has been upgraded to give more covered and heated accommodation. Just as important is that new and more economic vessels have been introduced to run alongside the veterans of the fleets. These vessels, such as the *Miss Cumbria* and *Lady Wakefield*, now offer an all-weather service.

Today, the steamers of the Lake District run a year-round service to satisfy the needs of changing visitor requirements. Steamer fleets are evolving to cater for new trends and needs as they have done since the 1850s. One thing that doesn't change is the dramatic, moody and ever-changing seasonal landscape of the Lake District. The very best way to sample this is aboard the deck of a traditional lake steamer!

1

The Furness Railway

Perhaps the greatest era for steamer services in the Lake District was in the years before the First World War, when the Furness Railway operated and marketed a wide range of tours and steamer routes upon the most popular lakes. (*Image by Abraham of Keswick*)

The real catalyst for the development of the Lake District steamers came with the Furness Railway. They opened a line from Ulverston to Lakeside on the shores of Windermere in 1869. This quickly led to the acquisition of the Windermere steamer fleet just three years later in 1872. The Furness Railway quickly embarked upon a programme of ordering new vessels with their own particular character. These steamers were of twin-screw design with low and long profiles. They were painted white to emphasise their grace and this tradition of having white hulls continues to this day. Some of these early steamers also had a canoe-style bow and an overhanging counter stern.

In 1895, Alfred Aslett became the new General Manager of the Furness Railway and immediately started to introduce new initiatives to boost the ailing railway as rail traffic to Barrow had been in decline. His strategy was bold and ambitious and had a lasting effect on the Lake District. The strategy was simple; Aslett transformed the Furness Railway into a tourist line. He reckoned that revenue could be significantly increased by maximising the tourist potential of the railway. In particular, he wanted to tap into the huge market offered by Blackpool on the other side of Morecambe Bay. The Lake District couldn't accommodate the working class tourists in its hotels and towns, but they would obviously enjoy a thrilling cruise across Morecambe Bay to Barrow and would thereby take a circular day tour using his services. Twenty different tours were offered to passengers whose Lakeland adventure utilised travelling by steamer, railway train and horse coach. The Furness Railway offered some of the first inclusive holiday tours in the UK. They offered people of Lancashire and beyond the chance to travel and admire the scenic beauty of the Lake District away from the grim everyday life of the mill town. The era of mass tourism in the English Lake District had begun.

The Furness Railway, from its inception, developed an ambitious and novel advertising programme for its Lake District services. This hand cart was one way that they advertised. It was pushed through the streets of Blackpool to promote the benefits of a cruise to Windermere and Coniston. Alfred Aslett was always on the lookout for novel means by which to advertise his Lake District services. In June 1910, Aslett purchased a model of *Gwalia* for £50 and then mounted it on wheels to be pushed around Blackpool to advertise his tours. Aslett was prominent in the first large-scale and effective advertising campaign for the English Lake District.

The *Lady Evelyn* departing on one of her cruises between Fleetwood and Barrow. *Lady Evelyn* was ordered from J. Scott & Co. It was hoped that she would be ready for service in 1900, but she was delayed briefly due to the financial difficulties of her builders. She was launched on 10 August, and was named after the wife of Mr Victor Cavendish, a director of the Furness Railway.

Lady Evelyn made her trial run at the end of 1900, with her inaugural passenger cruise taking place on Good Friday, 5 April 1901. *Lady Evelyn* was a relatively small paddle steamer being only 170 feet long. Her speed of 15 knots, allowed her to make the short 16-mile crossing between Fleetwood and Barrow in just one and a quarter hours. Two return trips were completed each day leaving Barrow at 9.00 a.m. and 1.45 p.m. and from Fleetwood at 10.45 a.m. and 6.00 p.m. Passenger numbers increased during the 1902 and 1903 seasons and it was decided to lengthen the *Lady Evelyn* by some 30 feet as a result. After this work, she could carry 714 passengers on a Class III certificate.

The *Lady Margaret* around 1905. In addition to rebuilding the *Lady Evelyn*, the Furness Railway purchased P & A Campbell's *Lady Margaret* in 1903. She was a large paddle steamer at 210 feet in length. Now with two steamers, the company were able to experiment with services and to expand their programme. The 1903 season was a great success. A grand total of 58,670 passengers had used the Fleetwood to Barrow service with a further 3,792 booking the circular tour ticket for the lake steamers.

The Barrow boat leaving Fleetwood with a full load of passengers. The Furness Railway advertised their Lake District services to a very wide market. Before the First World War for example, they exhibited at the White City in London. At one exhibition, over 8,000 visitors a day passed the stand, taking a precise 51,954 guide books and purchasing over 3,000 postcards. The postcards were sold in sets for 3*d* or 4*d*. They showed the scenic beauty of the Lake District as well as the Furness Railway lake steamers.

The *Philomel* was the next paddle steamer to join the Furness Railway fleet. She was originally owned by the General Steam Navigation Company of the River Thames and had been built in 1889. She was an unsuccessful steamer for the Furness Railway and soon gained the nickname 'Full-o-smell' by her regular passengers. She sailed with *Lady Evelyn* for the 1908 and 1909 seasons, but was advertised for sale at the end of that season. The Furness Railway stated that she had never been a success on the route and also required a new boiler at a cost of £5,000, which meant that it was uneconomic to operate her the following season.

After the unsuccessful Lake District career of the *Philomel*, the Furness Railway purchased the *Gwalia* from the Bristol Channel. She had an excellent operation speed of 19 knots and could easily cross between Fleetwood and Barrow in 45 minutes, carrying up to 1,015 passengers. She entered service on the route on Whit Saturday, 14 May 1910. *Gwalia* was soon after renamed *Lady Moyra* after Lady Moyra Cavendish. *Lady Moyra* was a significant success for the company.

THE LADY EVELYN LEAVING, FLEETWOOD.

FLEETWOOD.

In 1910, an amazing total of 128,000 passengers were carried on the Fleetwood to Barrow service. The most popular excursion offered by the Furness Railway was the 'Outer Circular Tour'. The starting point of the tour was Blackpool North Station. Passengers then travelled by train to Fleetwood before boarding a paddle steamer such as the *Lady Evelyn* for the crossing to Barrow.

Lady Moyra on the Fleetwood to Barrow run. On arrival at Barrow, a train left for the shores of Lake Windermere at Lakeside. At this point, passengers often enjoyed lunch in the splendid and vast refreshment rooms that were built by the Furness Railway on the pier. Diners were often serenaded by 'Bateson's Orchestral Band' led by Thomas Bateson on the cornet, with his wife on the violin and four other musicians. The ensemble had been formed by Mr Bateson's father in 1859 and continued serenading Windermere trippers until it ceased in 1915, due to the First World War. Thomas Bateson was very unhappy with this decision to stop playing as none of his ensemble were eligible for military service.

After luncheon, the majority of passengers boarded a steam yacht such as the *Tern*. From the pier at Lakeside, passengers generally sailed the full length of the lake to Ambleside. The next section of the tour was by horse-drawn coach to Coniston. A maximum of around 300 passengers could be carried on this section of the route. From Coniston, the connection was made to Barrow to connect with the paddle steamer. This was a truly magnificent day excursion at the modest cost of just eight shillings. It is hard to imagine today how exciting such a trip must have been to a Lancashire mill worker in the days before the First World War. (*J & C McCutcheon Collection*)

The service had everything in its favour from the start. The Furness Railway already owned the Ramsden Dock station at Barrow. This station was connected with the Furness main line from Carnforth to Barrow by a short branch line. Originally in 1865, the Furness Railway Company decided to build a branch line from Ulverston to Newby Bridge. A year later, on 16 July 1866, an Act of Parliament was obtained to start constructing the line. The branch line was quickly built and concluded with a purpose built steamer and train interchange at Lakeside. This remains to this day looking almost the same as the day when it was built. The first official train to work over the whole line was hauled by locomotive Number 21 and it ran from Barrow to a temporary station at Lakeside on 1 June 1869.

Swift arriving at Ambleside Pier around 1910 with the easily recognisable Furness Railway livery and white ensign flying at the bow. Note the grand style of dress and the carts of heavy luggage about to be placed on the steamer. The Victorians were very passionate about detail – even the gangway shows a flourish of style in its fancy iron end pieces. The Victorians were deeply passionate about the romance and beauty of the Lake District and did all that they could to exploit this. The lake steamers offered the perfect opportunity for people of all classes to experience the romance and beauty of the many lakes. And of course, this was experienced in steamers that used the style of the Victorian age in the main catalyst of the age – that of steam power.

In the final pre-war season of 1913, the passenger figures had gone up to an astonishing 179,000. It was rumoured at the time that a new and superior steamer capable of carrying up to 1,500 passengers was being contemplated on the Fleetwood to Barrow run. The 1914 season continued as planned, but after the declaration of war in August 1914, services stopped as the *Lady Evelyn* and *Lady Moyra* were requisitioned for war service as minesweepers.

Britannia was a striking vessel and was built by Seath of Rutherglen in 1879 for the private use of Colonel Ridealgh. She was purchased by the Furness Railway in 1907 as a Directors' yacht, as well as for conveying private charters around the lake in the years before the First World War. *Britannia* could carry up to 122 passengers in great comfort. 'Bateson's Orchestra Band' often played during these cruises. Sometimes, chartered pleasure steamers from the Fylde coast would arrange for passengers to be taken onwards from Barrow to Lakeside to embark upon the *Britannia* for more intimate private cruises. *Britannia* was laid up in 1915 and scrapped in 1919. She was one of the most distinctive steamers that ever plied the lake.

The last of the coal-fired pleasure steamers was commissioned in 1899 by the Furness Railway. *Swift* was launched in 1900 at a cost of £9,500. Powered by steam-compound engines, she could carry up to 781 passengers. *Swift* sailed as a steam vessel until 1956 when her boiler burst. Soon after, British Railways installed Glennifer diesel engines. She continued in service until 1981, when she was laid up at Lakeside. Sadly, after attempts were made to preserve her had failed, she was broken up in 1999.

Posters produced by the Furness Railway were very distinctive and beautifully designed. They managed to capture the atmosphere of the lakes and their steamers.

The Coniston tour was known as the 'Inner Circle Tour' and included the usual steamer from Fleetwood to Barrow, then a train to Greenodd, followed by a horse-drawn coach from Greenodd to Lake Bank, and then a delightful cruise on *Gondola* to Waterhead. A train was then taken back from Coniston to Barrow and then onwards to Fleetwood.

The first *Swan* on Windermere was built by T. B. Seath for the Furness Railway and cost £4,000 to build. Her claim to fame was that she was the very first screw vessel on Windermere. In some ways she looked like a steam yacht, but could be distinguished by her promenade deck above her saloon. This was quite an innovation at the time and made her a very handsome steamer. Note the tall and thin funnel that was a feature of most of the Victorian steamers. If you look closely, you will notice the large carved swan sitting upon the bow.

The Furness Railway's *Swift* arriving at Ambleside Pier around 1910. Lakeside and Ambleside were the main piers on Windermere at the time. Windermere is England's largest lake. It is perhaps incorrect to refer to this stunning stretch of water as 'Lake Windermere', as a 'mere' is another word for 'lake'. The name 'Windermere' is derived from the Old Norse 'Onundar Myrr'.

An atmospheric image showing the *Lady of the Lake* arriving at Lake Bank Pier on Coniston. *Lady of the Lake* had been built many hundreds of miles away at the famed Southampton yard of John Thorneycroft and was transported to Waterhead for assembly. *Lady of the Lake* was launched by Miss Williamson. Like *Gondola*, *Lady of the Lake* was part of the Furness Railway's 'Inner Circle Tour', as a replacement for the ageing *Gondola*. But after public opposition, *Gondola* was never withdrawn. Captain Hamill became *Lady of the Lake*'s first master in 1908, after being master of *Gondola* for around fifty years.

Gondola was built by Jones Quiggan & Company at Liverpool. At 42 tons, she had a length of 84 feet, a width of just over 14 feet and a depth of 3 feet. The elegant and ornate bow of the *Gondola* had the Duke of Devonshire's coronet on it with a gilded serpent wrapped round it. The Duke of Devonshire was the chairman of the local railway company. *Gondola* was the perfect marriage of Venetian gondola and English steam yacht. The first class saloon was luxuriously decorated in walnut with sumptuous upholstery and gilded Corinthian columns alongside the windows.

The *Gondola* moored next to *Lady of the Lake* on Coniston around 1910, with passengers about to embark on the next leg of their adventure.

If you look at this and other postcards and photographs of the Furness Railway steamers, you will notice that they always flew the white ensign. This of course was only allowable aboard ships of the Royal Navy and the Furness Railway was technically breaking the law by not flying the usual red ensign.

At the shore end of the pier shown in this image, is a small building now known as 'The Bluebird Café'. This building is yet another reminder of the heyday of the Furness Railway and would have been familiar to the people shown in this image before the First World War.

Gondola being launched on Coniston. Arther Ransome is a name that is synonymous with the Lake District and its steamers. The lake in his most famous and well-loved book, *Swallows and Amazons*, is an amalgam of Coniston Water and Windermere. Belle Isle on Windermere became the Swallows' Long Island and Silver Holme became Cormorant Island. The Furness Railway's *Gondola* on Coniston Water is said by many to be the model for Captain Flint's house boat. The link for this went back to Arthur Ransome's childhood, when the captain allowed him to steer the steamer on its cruises on Coniston. (*J & C McCutcheon Collection*)

Gondola shown in a peaceful scene on Coniston, with the Waterhead Hotel in the distance, around 1905. The Waterhead Hotel welcomed many guests of John Ruskin who lived nearby. One well-known guest was Charles Darwin. *Gondola*'s engine was originally made up of two cylinders, with one either side of the locomotive-type boiler. Originally, fumes from the coke used to fire the vessel and the exhaust steam was taken out to the stern. A raked funnel was later added to improve the workings of the engine.

The *Gondola*, at the venerable age of seventy-six, went into retirement in the mid-1930s. (*J & C McCutcheon Collection*)

A fine view showing the elegant lines of *Gondola*. Note the crew member with the wooden pole and rowing boat for going ashore at the stern. It is rumoured that *Gondola* was modelled on the elegant looking steamers on the Italian lakes and obviously echoes the watercraft of Venice. A prominent director of the Furness Railway, who lived in nearby Barrow-in-Furness, had visited Italy and may have got personal inspiration for the unique and beautiful *Gondola* on Coniston.

Lady of the Lake – a grand steamer of the Furness Railway fleet in the days before the First World War. The Furness Railway guide for 1915 continued to advertise the Fleetwood to Barrow service, but the advertisement was overprinted 'Deferred until further notice'. Both paddle steamers survived the conflict and most assumed that full service would be resumed in 1919. However, a brief announcement was made instead to say that sailings would not recommence as the service had never been profitable and that conditions had changed after the First World War. Coincidentally, Alfred Aslett, the architect of the steamer service, retired at this time. At first it was hoped that the Blackpool Passenger Steamboat Company would consider taking up the Barrow to Fleetwood service, but this never happened apart from a few Sunday and Bank Holiday sailings in 1919. Thus both *Lady Evelyn* and *Lady Moyra* were duly sold and the 'Lakeland Connection' of the Furness Railway ceased. The lake steamers thankfully survived.

A scene at Coniston with *Gondola* and *Lady of the Lake* during the heyday of the Furness Railway. Note the helmsman at the open wheel of the *Gondola*. The Furness Railway, under the management of Alfred Aslett, managed to create an imaginative and effective service of steamers to supply the Lake District with ever increasing numbers of visitor. The service, albeit short lived, provided a great legacy that survives to this day. The piers, steamers and routes built and managed by the Furness Railway have, almost a century after its heyday, continued to provide enjoyment to new generations of trippers. Two of the lake steamers, *Gondola* and *Tern*, provide a strong link back to those early and glorious years of Lake District steamers.

2

Lake Windermere

Lake Windermere has always been a popular destination for day-trippers wanting a lake-steamer cruise. The *Swan*, *Teal* and *Tern*, along with a host of smaller vessels, carry on the great tradition started in Victorian times. (*J & C McCutcheon Collection*)

An early view showing Lakeside Pier. The Kendal to Windermere Railway opened in 1847. The branch attracted many holidaymakers and in its first full year carried 120,000 passengers. Previous to this, the lake had probably seen little more than the odd rowing boat. Now, paddle steamers began to exploit the lake and to transport many hundreds of passengers to see the great beauties of the lake and to visit the fast-growing towns and villages. Windermere was now ready for an explosion of tourism.

The Windermere Iron Steamboat Company was formed as a rival to the Windermere Steam Yacht Company. They operated *Fire Fly* and *Dragon Fly*. By the mid-1850s, this newer company merged with the Windermere Steam Yacht Company to form the Windermere United Steam Yacht Company in 1858. Services in the 1860s saw many changes. In 1866, the *Rothay* saw entry into service. By this time, the *Lord of the Isles* had been destroyed in 1850 and *Lady of the Lake* had been withdrawn a few years earlier.

By the late 1860s, the Furness Railway had created a branch line to Newby Bridge, towards the southern end of the lake. In 1869, a new pier and adjacent station and refreshment buildings were built at Lakeside. This development at the quieter southern end of the lake provided the spark that would see tourism explode on England's premier lake. By this time a greater number of tourists than ever before were able to sample the panoramic delights of Wordworth's Lake District by means of the railway and lake steamer – two of the great inventions of the Victorian age. There were basically two kinds of tourist. Some were wealthy mill owners and industrialists who had become wealthy because of the industrialisation of the Victorian age. The others were an up and coming group of people that would one day cause the Lakes to explode with tourism. These were the working classes that toiled in the mills and who were now able, albeit in a very limited sense, to explore and appreciate the beauty and freedom of the Lakes – a world far away from the industrial mills of Lancashire and Yorkshire.

Within five years the Furness Railway had taken over the steamer services. With a firm and large base at Lakeside, they were able to run a regular steamer service between Lakeside, Bowness and Ambleside – a service that remains and flourishes to this day. (*J & C McCutcheon Collection*)

The steam ferry across Windermere in around 1904. The Windermere ferry operates between Sawrey and Cockshot Point close to Bowness. Before the steam ferries, passengers as well as goods were rowed across. This original ferry remained at the lakeside until the mid-1930s, as it was sometimes used as a reserve means of crossing the lake if the steam ferry was out of service. The first steam ferries appeared around the late 1860s. The number of horse vehicles that could be carried was somewhat limited, but was made up by the number of passengers carried in and on top of the coaches! Many of the lady passengers hold parasols above them to protect themselves from the sun.

Bowness. Ferry Nab.

An atmospheric and quiet view of the Windermere ferry with the ferry laden with carts and goods in the days before the motor car became king. Ferry operators, including John Braithwaite of Bowness, originally rowed passengers up and down Windermere, exchanging people and goods at the Hawkshead Ferry.

The Furness Railway was synonymous with the expansion and the 'Golden Age' of the Windermere lake fleet. Typical of their steamers was the *Swift*. This was a product of the prolific Rutherglen yard of T. B. Seath. One wonders whether they constructed vessels for anywhere other than the English Lake District. She was built in 1900 and had a larger capacity (781 passengers) than her predecessor *Tern*. The *Rothay* of 1866 was the last paddle steamer on Lake Windermere and was withdrawn in around 1900 and replaced by the screw steamer *Swift*.

The elegant first *Swan* (predecessor of the present *Swan*) at Loughrigg, viewed from Waterhead around 1920. She was the largest steamer of the Victorian fleet and entered service in 1869. *Swan* was 111 feet long and could accommodate up to 442 passengers. *Swan* cost £4,000 to build and was scrapped by the LMS in 1938. This image shows the beautiful long profile of the *Swan* with an absence of deck shelters and plenty of open deck to admire the Lakeland landscape.

Tern approaching Waterhead Pier. Harriet Martineau was shocked by the inhabitants of Ambleside when she set up home there. She was shocked by the sheer dirt, drunkenness and overcrowding of the village. On closer inspection, she found that young men rarely took a bath and a local superstition was that if a baby had its hands and arms washed before the age of six months it was considered to be very bad luck! One wonders what the early trippers made of the locals. When *Tern* entered service in 1891, she was the largest steamer in service on Windermere and cost £5,000 to build by Forrest & Sons of Wivenhoe in Essex. The firm of Forrest had originally come from London and specialised in 'self assembly' steamers such as *Tern*. Apart from the *Tern*, Forrest & Sons also built the steam launch *Otto* on Windermere. (*Image by Abraham of Keswick*)

The *Teal* was built for service on Lake Windermere in 1879 by the Barrow Shipbuilding Company. She was 100 feet long, 14 feet wide and had a depth of 3.6 feet. When built, she could carry 336 passengers.

An early view at Bowness, with the Old England Hotel in the distance. The lake steamer services did have another important function at the time. The wealthy industrialists and landowners of the Victorian boom had built fine houses along the shores of Lake Windermere. They needed steamer services that would help them to commute to their mills and factories as well as to dinner parties and to nearby towns and villages for provisions. Such wealthy people were no longer willing to accept limited or no transport facilities. Instead, they required fast and reliable steamer services linking in with that great invention of the Victorian age – the railway.

Swift has the distinction of being the last pleasure steamer built by Seath of Rutherglen and has a certain similarity to the *Sir Walter Scott* on Lake Katrine in Scotland, which was built in the same year. *Swift* was 150 feet long, with a width of 21 feet and depth of just over 10 feet.

Esperance at the Ferry Hotel Pier in around 1920. *Esperance* was owned by the Ferry Hotel at the time and was used to carry visitors to the hotel for polite afternoon teas. The Ferry Hotel's guests were also often conveyed for morning worship aboard the *Esperance* to the church at Wray. There is some disagreement as to whether the *Esperance* or *Gondola* was the model for Captain Flint's houseboat in *Swallows and Amazons*. *Esperance* was, however, used by the BBC for a television adaptation of the famous Lakeland book. (*Image by Abraham of Keswick*)

A London & North Western Railway postcard showing the *Swift* on Lake Windermere. *Swift* was the largest of the early Windermere steamers at 150 feet in length. Wordsworth was ultra-sensitive to the mere mention of technology and steam power into his beloved Lake District. He wrote in 1844 that '... the staple of the district is, in fact, its beauty and its character of seclusion'. He argued that the best way to see and admire the lakes was on foot and by climbing a mountain. When you look at this image it is easy to think that he was wrong.

An atmospheric view of *Tern* arriving at Bowness in around 1920. A good queue of passengers can be seen at the pier head. The many boathouses that lined the lake can be seen towards the left of the image.

Ambleside from Loughrigg.

Bridge House, Ambleside.

Waterhead, Lake Windermere

Win. 74.

William Wordsworth was perhaps the greatest promoter of the English Lake District. During his lifetime, the area was a haven for peace and quiet and Wordsworth fought any schemes to exploit the natural charm of the area and to thereby spoil its charms. Paradoxically, William Wordsworth has been perhaps one of the greatest catalysts to exploit the tourist potential of the Lake District. The crowded roads and busy towns are, in many respects, a reflection of how people have enjoyed his work over the years.

Swift embarking passengers at Bowness Pier. The white ensign of the Furness Railway can be seen at the bow indicating that this image was taken during the Furness Railway years, which ended in the early 1920s with the creation of the 'Big Four' railway companies.

Cygnet cruising on Lake Windermere during her LMS years.

A nostalgic look back at the quieter days of horse transport on the Windermere ferry. The towns and villages of the Lake District grew substantially with the coming of the railways. Public houses, lodging houses, hotels and shops were built to cater for the growing needs of visitors. The population of Windermere and Bowness increased from 2,085 in 1851 to 4,613 in 1891. The ferries and steamers, therefore, had a major role in ferrying goods, livestock and people between the settlements.

In the days before the steam-powered ferries, people were rowed by two oarsmen and in bad weather this was increased to four. Horses was regularly carried and were placed in the centre of the ferry to stop them going overboard in bad weather. Livestock, carriages, carts and an assortment of goods accompanied the human load. The chains operating the ferry can be clearly seen in this photograph, which dates from around 1914. (*J & C McCutcheon Collection*)

The Furness Railway laid up the *Cygnet* during the First World War. In 1923, she changed radically when her old and very smooth running steam engines were changed to paraffin engines. These were noisy and shook a great deal. *Cygnet* continued to cruise on Windermere until the mid-1950s. At that time it was hoped that she would see further service, but instead remained rotting before being broken up around 1970. *Cygnet* is shown here at Lakeside on 18 September 1953.

Surprisingly, not everyone has always liked the Lake District and steamers. The great writer Charles Dickens once described Ambleside as: 'Round Ambleside you will indeed find hills and waterfalls – decked with greasy sandwich papers and porter bottles, and the hills echo with the whistles of the Windermere steamers, brass bands play under your hotel windows, char-a-bancs, wagonettes and brakes of all colours rattle about with cargoes of tourists who have been "doing" some favourite round. Touts pester you in the streets and in the hotel coffee room you overhear a gentleman asks angrily, "Why don't they build an 'ut on 'elvellyn they've got one on Snowdon.' (*Image by Abraham of Keswick*)

An Edwardian scene at Bowness. The first known steamer built for the English Lake District was the *Lady of the Lake* in 1845. She was constructed of wood and was operated by the Windermere Steam Yacht Company. She plied between Newby Bridge on the River Leven to Ambleside. This distance of 11 miles took about an hour and a quarter by steamer – far quicker than the journey by horse or coach. Other lake vessels often took over three hours and therefore lost business quite quickly. The success of *Lady of the Lake* in her first year meant that a second steamer was quickly ordered. The *Lord of the Isles* was launched at Newby Bridge in 1846.

Tern is a unique survivor on Windermere. She is just over 140 feet long, 18 feet wide and with a depth of 3.6 feet. She has a capacity of 608. Originally she was a two-class steamer.

Tern departing from Bowness Pier. Few could have realised that when *Tern* entered service towards the end of the Victorian era she would become the longest serving of all Windermere steamers by continuing to cruise up and down the lake into the twenty-first century. (*J & C McCutcheon Collection*)

Swift approaching the pier at Bowness in around 1920. When do you think the first ferry operated on Windermere? It is known that the monks of Furness Abbey were the first to operate a licensed cargo boat in the thirteenth century. This connected with a trading route between Hawkshead and Kendal. It later became known as the 'Horse Ferry'. Some 300 years later, the first steam service was inaugurated.

Passengers enjoying a cruise aboard a Windermere steamer on 7 June 1936. It is interesting to note how formal the passengers look with the two ladies wearing fox furs and all wearing hats of some kind. Steamer services had reached a pinnacle of perfection under the direction of the Furness Railway. The beautiful, stylish and quiet steamers combined with excellent railways connections, excellent piers and shore facilities. There was also a plentiful supply of passengers hungry for a lake cruise.

The *Swan* approaching a pier on Windermere in 1932, with plenty of steam issuing from her. The first *Swan* had a charming and slender funnel placed midships. It was said that she had a sound rather like a puffing railway locomotive. She was 141.7 feet long, had a width of 17 feet and a depth of 3.3 feet. She could carry a surprising 442 passengers.

396. Belsfield Hotel from the Pier, Bowness

The Belsfield Hotel, shown here above the lake at Bowness, was once the impressive home of Henry Schneider who was chairman of the Barrow Steelworks. *Esperance* is reputed to be the first twin-screw yacht to be built in Britain. She was ordered by Schneider, who was nicknamed the 'Iron Man' due to him having made his fortune in the iron ore industry of West Cumbria. Money for her construction was therefore plentiful. *Esperance* was delivered from the Clyde to Barrow-in-Furness and then by train to Lakeside. Special arrangements had to be made under the many railway bridges to ensure that the steamer fitted through the narrow aperture. Schneider ensured that only the highest grade of iron was used in her construction. To add to her visual impact, the riveting was countersunk to give a very smooth finish to the hull. Schneider used *Esperance* on a daily basis by travelling on her from his residence in Bowness to Lakeside and then onwards to his office by train. His rather luxurious means of getting to work wasn't too uncommon as a large number of wealthy industrialists built residences on the banks of Lake Windermere. Each day Schneider enjoyed breakfast aboard *Esperance* on the way to Lakeside. He then transferred to the steam train to Barrow to work. As a director of the railway, he had the further luxury of travelling in a private carriage. *Esperance* was Seath's 99th ship and was constructed in 1869. (*Image by Abraham of Keswick*)

You can really appreciate the canoe-like bow of the *Tern* from this photograph. This was a common feature of Victorian Lake District steamers. The wooden carving of the tern can be clearly admired. The *Tern* is now the oldest pleasure steamer on Windermere dating back to 1891. The use of bird names became the norm for the Windermere fleet during the great Victorian expansion of the fleet. (*J & C McCutcheon Collection*)

A passenger poses at the wheel of the *Swift* on Windermere around 1932. The smart LMS lifebuoys can be appreciated along with her funnel and steam whistle. The funnel was changed to one of a less pleasing oval shape later in her career.

STEAMER PIER, LAKESIDE

S.626

The Furness Railway had great expertise in providing everything that the tripper needed. The interchange at Lakeside provided a stunning example of how the Victorian transport system came together and provided luxury and facilities to entice passengers back on future visits. The glass-topped refreshment room above the pier allowed waiting passengers to get their first glimpse of the lake as well as taking their money for luncheons, teas and souvenirs. The people behind the Furness Railway were great businessmen.

A gentleman wearing typical 1930s holiday-wear posing on the open bridge of the *Swift* in 1932. It would be difficult to find a better image showing the bridge with its wheel and telegraph. The poor master and helmsman only have a slender bench to sit upon. The chains from the wheel can also be seen running down into the engine room below. In addition, the cable running from the steam whistle to the railing behind the man is visible.

With the expansion of steam launches and yachts on Windermere, a number of local boat builders set up business. The firms of Shepherds, Brockbank's and Borwicks catered for these small and beautifully crafted steamers. By spending their working lives on Windermere they have had extremely long lives.

Cygnet and *Teal* at Ambleside in their heyday. The contract to build these two traditional Victorian steamers was awarded to the Barrow Shipbuilding Company and they had been launched at Lakeside in 1879. They cost around £3,400 each to build.

By the mid-1930s, the large and powerful London, Midland & Scottish Railway (who had inherited the Furness Railway fleet) wanted to make changes on Windermere. The changes were revolutionary and somewhat typical of the new streamlined age. They immediately set about scrapping two of the old steamers and then converted two more to motor vessels. However, the biggest change was the introduction of two new splendid and very large motor ships – the *Teal* of 1936 and the *Swan* of 1938. These two new steamers had three decks of passenger accommodation and were quite revolutionary for the time. *Teal* proved so popular that the following year, the London, Midland & Scottish Railway commissioned a sister ship named the *Swan*. She was also constructed by Vickers Armstrong at Barrow. *Swan* made her maiden voyage on 24 June 1938, when she carried delegates to attend the 37th Annual Conference of the Municipal Tramways and Transport Association on a charter from Lakeside Pier.

A special view of *Teal* arriving at Lakeside for the first time, although this time it is on train tracks and not the waters of Lake Windermere. *Teal* (yard number 715) was delivered in sections by LMS locomotive from Barrow to Lakeside station, where she was unloaded and built on the slipway at the side of the lake. (*Dock Museum* (*Image 1903*))

Teal under construction on the slipway at Lakeside in 1936, looking towards Lake Windermere (after transportation of sections from Barrow). Note that someone has cheekily written *Queen Mary II* on the side of the hull in recognition of the Cunard liner that entered service in the same year. Also note the sidings built to get the locomotive and its ship parts as close as possible to *Teal* on the slipway. (*Dock Museum* (*Image 1906*))

A view of the guests, including the sponsor, Miss Harris, along with Commander Craven arriving for the launch ceremony of the *Teal* on 4 July 1936. (*Dock Museum* (*Image 1921*))

The climax of activity for the London, Midlands & Scottish Railway's operation of Lakeland steamers came with the construction of the large and splendid *Teal* in 1936 and *Swan* in 1938. These vessels were unlike any other Lakeland vessels of the time and have survived changing tastes and trends for almost eighty years. (*J & C McCutcheon Collection*)

The Teal, Lake Windermere.   S.5u

By Vickers standards, *Teal* was a small ship at 250 tons and could accommodate up to 877 passengers. She operated as a two-class ship, with first and third class accommodation over three decks. Her interiors were sleek, stylish and modern to reflect the 1930s style. (*J & C McCutcheon Collection*)

Teal was followed soon after by the *Swan*. She was a similar vessel, built again at Barrow. The *Teal* and *Swan* became the flagship LMS steamers of the 1930s. You can appreciate the wide-open deck of these 1930s steamers from this image. The bridge and top deck are open with no protection from the rain. While this was wonderful in fine sunny weather, it was less than satisfactory in inclement weather. Note the canvas dodgers on the rails protecting passengers from cold breezes. (*J & C McCutcheon Collection*)

The *Teal* at Waterhead on Lake Windermere. Windermere is the largest lake in England with a length of 10.5 miles. The largest island is Belle Isle. If you wanted to walk around the whole of Windermere instead of cruising on it, you would walk a distance of 27 miles. Lake Windermere is classed as a public highway. In past centuries, it supported commercial traffic associated with slate and copper mining, timber, wool and fishing.

The *Teal* arriving at Bowness with a very full load of passengers around the 1930s, soon after entering service. Most of the passengers are wearing the obligatory 1930s hat. *Teal* was 142 feet long with a breadth of 25 feet. Her regular speed was 11 knots and could carry up to 877 passengers.

A scene that all motorists have experienced while visiting Windermere has to be the never-ending queue of traffic waiting for the ferry to cross the lake between Sawrey to Cockshot Point. In this inter-war view, note the grand ladies carrying parasols to shield themselves from the sun and the top-hatted carriage driver with his horse. (*Image by Abraham of Keswick*) (*J & C McCutcheon Collection*)

Tern departing from Bowness Bay around the time when *Swan* and *Teal* were introduced. The low canoe-shaped fore deck on the *Tern* was originally used exclusively by first-class passengers. This gave them a wonderful close view of the water of the lake. Third-class passengers were crammed on benches aboard the top deck with lesser views of the lake. *Tern* was very different to the newer *Swan* and *Teal*, although the three of them have all survived some eighty years later. (*J & C McCutcheon Collection*)

A 1930s view of the pier at Bowness. Nowadays, the beautifully varnished and traditional Windermere launches, such as *Queen of the Lake*, offer shorter cruises around the lake to places such as Brockhole and Wray towards the northern end of Windermere. These cruises allow close views of the hidden bays and many fine large houses that surround the lake. Routes for these launches now allow passengers to cross the lake and to then travel onwards by minibus to Beatrix Potter country at Hawkshead. Traditional wooden-varnished rowing boats can be seen on the shingle in the foreground.

A steamer at Waterhead during the 1930s. The northern terminus of the Windermere steamer service is at Waterhead. The landing stage and offices are situated a short distance from the town centre of Ambleside. Ambleside, like other Lake District towns, rapidly expanded as a result of the tourist influx from the 1860s onwards.

A fine view showing one of the traditional wooden-varnished launches on Windermere.

The promenade at Ambleside on Lake Windermere with a wide variety of launches and rowing boats.

The second of the large new steamers to be built for service on Windermere by the LMS was *Swan*. *Swan* is shown here being launched at Lakeside on 10 June 1938. (*Dock Museum (Image 1955)*)

A view of *Swan*'s splendid promenade deck pictured at Lakeside in June 1938. It shows, in the most perfect of weather, how wonderful this wide-open deck could be for passengers. Note the open bridge, which must have been a splendid vantage platform for the master in glorious sunshine. Unfortunately, the often-wet Lakeland weather made this wonderful feature of the 1930s *Swan* less attractive in rain and wind. (*Dock Museum* (*Image 1959*))

A model of the *Swan* showing her original condition when built in 1938 by Vickers Armstrong of Barrow. One wonders whether the weather at the time was always sunny and dry, as from this model you will see that originally she had an open bridge (with canvas dodgers) and top deck. You can also appreciate the large windows of the Observation Lounge below the bridge, offering vast panoramic views of the lake and mountains. (*J & C McCutcheon Collection*)

Swan's stylish Sun Lounge with stairs leading down to the First Class Lounge. Note the Lloyd Loom chairs – a pre-requisite of any 1930s steamer interior. Few photographs exist of the interior of the Lake District steamers. The modern and quite plain 1930s interior was a great contrast with the often darker Victorian interiors of the rest of the Windermere steamer fleet. (*Dock Museum* (*Image 1956*))

A view of *Swan*'s main deck from the bridge while she was berthed at Lakeside Pier in June 1938. *Swift* and another steamer are berthed ahead of *Swan*. Note the details of *Swan*'s deck, such as the seating and livery. (*Dock Museum* (*Image 1961*))

Swan cruising during the early part of her career. The storm clouds of the Second World War appeared just as *Swan* entered service. After the cessation of hostilities in 1945, the steamer scene on England's greatest lake carried on almost as before. This was in stark contrast to what was happening elsewhere with steamer fleets. The then veteran *Cygnet* had been used for occasional charter and relief work until the Second World War. In 1947, she was used during the summer season when government austerity regulations meant that a temporary halt to the running of the coal-fired steamers was implemented. (*J & C McCutcheon Collection*)

Teal cruising on Windermere in August 1952. A decade later, on 1 January 1963, the British Railways Board, under the chairmanship of Dr Beeching, assumed responsibility from the British Transport Commission for the management of the Windermere lake steamers. Two notable figures were involved with the operation of the Windermere fleet at this time. Captain A. E. Willmott DSC was the District Marine Manager and Harbour Master at Heysham. He was helped locally by his Marine Engineer Foreman, Richard Jones. He served some thirty-two years with the Windermere fleet. (*J & C McCutcheon Collection*)

This 1950s view shows the *Swan* arriving at the former Furness Railway station and pier at Lakeside. Amazingly, the pier and facilities at Lakeside have survived intact from the days of the Furness Railway. (*J & C McCutcheon Collection*)

During the inter-war years, there were normally four steamers operating during the main summer season on Windermere. Usually, another was placed on standby to take up service if required. If the four main steamers were operating during this period, an amazing total of 3,146 passengers could be carried on the lake at any one time. The highest number could be carried on the *Teal* (877), with the least number being carried on the *Tern* (633).

Up until the 1950s, Lakeside was the most popular departure point for Windermere steamer trips as it had a good rail link alongside the pier. By the late 1940s, as lake steamer trade quickly regained pre-war levels, it soon became clear that the emergence of the motor car meant that Bowness, with its good road links, was making it the most popular departure point. This was finally cemented with the closure of the British Railways line at Lakeside in 1965. (*Image by Abraham of Keswick*) (*J & C McCutcheon Collection*)

The commercial use of passenger launches on Windermere flourished during the inter-war years. By the start of the Second World War, there were around thirty passenger launches working at Bowness. After the Second World War, larger launches were introduced on Windermere. They included *Sunflower II* (1949), *Queen of the Lake* (1949) and *Princess of the Lake* (1950). Many of the small, twelve-seater craft became uneconomic and were withdrawn from service. (*J & C McCutcheon Collection*)

Since Victorian times the emphasis on the use of lake steamers has changed a great deal. Mail, livestock, goods and local people are now transported by road instead. The pleasure steamers have the equally important role of transporting tourists, which now provides the main income source for most of the Lake District. Around 8.3 million day visitors now visit the Lake District every year. Some 89 per cent of these visitors arrive by car.

Osprey and *Shamrock* were some of the oldest Windermere steam launches and were built by Shepherds, a local boatbuilding firm.

The *Drake* arrived on Windermere in 1954. Two ferries had preceded her; the first was introduced in 1870 and the second one in 1915. Allsops of Lytham in Lancashire built the *Drake* and she was the last boat to be built there before they closed. *Drake* was converted to diesel in 1960, just six years after she entered service. *Drake* had a relatively short life on Windermere as she was taken out of service in 1990. Her time on the lake coincided with the huge explosion in motor car usage. Her limited amount of space for cars meant that a new ferry had to be built. (*J & C McCutcheon Collection*)

Drake operating the chain ferry service during the 1950s. The chain car ferry makes around three return trips every hour for around twelve hours a day. It provides a short-cut for traffic between Bowness and Hawkshead. (*J & C McCutcheon Collection*)

158. Windermere Ferry Boat "Drake".

Drake operating the Windermere car and passenger ferry around 1955. The *Mallard* now provides the ferry service across Windermere beneath Bowness. She replaced the *Drake* and was built in 1990 at Borth in North Wales. Surprisingly, she can carry around 100 passengers and around eighteen cars or other vehicles. *Mallard* cannot really be claimed to be a pleasure boat due to her function of providing a service to make getting from A to B faster. However, she does offer a service firmly in the past. Her passengers can still enjoy the scenic splendours of Lake Windermere from her deck with the added luxury of heated passenger accommodation. (*Image by Abraham of Keswick*)

WINDERMERE, BELLE ISLE AND BOWNESS   9026.

Belle Isle is the largest of the islands on Windermere and has always been a part of the itinerary for steamer cruises. At three quarters of a mile long it almost cuts the lake in half. In the middle of Belle Isle is a round house, which was built in 1774. The Curwen family lived there for many years. Twelve densely-wooded islands are situated on Windermere. Bowness can be seen in the distance of this image. (*Image by Abraham of Keswick*)

Swan and *Teal* alongside Lakeside Pier in around 1938. Passenger numbers increased in the years immediately after the Second World War. London, Midland & Scottish Railway steamer operations, including the Windermere Steamer fleet, passed to the ownership of the British Transport Commission on 1 January 1948, when the railway companies were nationalised. (*J & C McCutcheon Collection*)

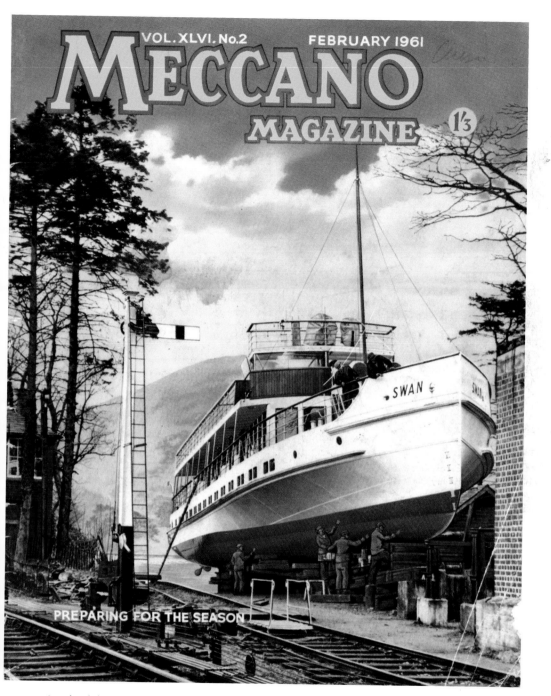

VOL. XLVI. No.2   FEBRUARY 1961

MECCANO

MAGAZINE

1/3

PREPARING FOR THE SEASON

1 A splendid cover from *The Meccano Magazine* of February 1961, showing the Windermere based *Swan* being painted ready for the summer season while on the slipway at Lakeside. Note the railway track adjacent to the steamer. This was used to transport the *Swan* to the lake in sections during the mid-1930s. She was then built on this slipway. (*J & C McCutcheon Collection*)

The Ferry Crossing. Windermere.

2 Below Bowness and opposite Claife, Windermere narrows to just 560 yards. Originally, the monks of Furness Abbey owned and operated the first crossing here in the fourteenth century and early passengers had to row themselves across the lake at this point. Later, as people needed to access markets and newly built towns and villages, it became necessary to provide proper ferries that enabled livestock and goods to be transported. During the nineteenth century, steam propulsion came into use and made a huge difference until it was superseded by the diesel-powered *Drake* in around 1960. This image shows the original steam ferry on the crossing over Windermere. (*J & C McCutcheon Collection*)

3 The *Cygnet* cruising on Windermere around 1910. *Cygnet* was built at a cost of £3,400 by the Barrow Shipbuilding Company. She was quite similar to her sister the *Swan*. Perhaps one of the most unusual features of the *Cygnet* was having the engine control levers positioned on the bridge.

CONISTON LAKE & GONDOLA

4 *Gondola* is now regarded by almost everyone as being a beautiful, graceful and very unique steamer. In the past, some have been less than complimentary. She was once described as 'a cross between a floating cucumber and submarine' and as a 'floating canoe!'

5 Steamer alongside Pooley Bridge with Soulby Fell in the background. During the next century, *Lady of the Lake* sank during the 1950s at Pooley Bridge during a gale. She was quickly pumped out by the fire brigade and returned to service. She again escaped destruction in 1965, when a fire broke out in workshops during her winter lay-up. She was severely damaged during the fire and it took many years and over £60,000 to restore her.

6 *Raven* at Patterdale. The Ullswater steamers *Lady of the Lake* and *Raven* were built by the respected Clyde firm of Thomas Bollin Seath of Rutherglen. Among other steamers built at Seath's yard were yachts built for the King of Siam and the King of Burma. At least eight steamers built for service in the Lake District were built by Seath of Rutherglen.

7 *Dolly* was built around 1850 and was removed around 1890 from Windermere to Ullswater. Unfortunately, she sank during the big freeze on 21 February 1895. A local story stated that a local woman was waiting for her baby to be born and noticed *Dolly* the evening before. On the following day and after the birth, *Dolly* had sunk. It wasn't until 1962 that the boat was located by divers from the Furness Sub Aqua Club. *Dolly* was then taken back to Windermere for eventual restoration. When she left Windermere in 1890, she was hauled by horse or steam-driven wagon. Some seventy-two years later she was moved by more efficient means.

8 The *Raven* alongside Glenridding Pier. It is a great surprise to visitors in the twenty-first century to find out that Glenridding was, until 1962, when lead mining ceased at Greenside, one of the most important mining villages in the UK. The pier at Glenridding is now an impressive and modern visitor centre for users of the Ullswater steamers with shop, café and displays. This is far removed from the humble facilities shown in this view.
(*J & C McCutcheon Collection*)

9 A 1960s view showing the old and the new – the varnished wood of the Lake Windermere ferry and the modern motor car.

10 A view of Lakeside during the Furness Railway era. The steamer at the front is the *Raven*. The *Raven* was yet another steamer built by Seath of Rutherglen in 1871. She was built for the Furness Railway and cost the remarkably small sum of £1,400. Her role was different to other steamers in that her role was to work and not to convey passengers. She was a cargo steamer used to transport all sorts of goods around the Windermere piers and in particular villages on the west side that were not easily accessible by other means. At times she acted as an ice breaker, but rarely conveyed passengers around the lake. *Raven* was named after the ravens that fed Elijah when he was in the wilderness in the bible. Windermere's *Raven* finished her career in 1922 and then became an experimental vessel for Armstrong Vickers so that they could study mine-laying techniques. After many years of neglect and laying in a sunken state, she was rescued by the Windermere Steamboat Museum for preservation

11 The pier at Lakeside with two steamers alongside it. After the nationalisation of the railways to form British Railways in 1948, the London Midland Region of this new body took over management of the Windermere steamers. Little changed until 1970, when Sealink took over the maritime arm of British Rail. By that time, British Rail had cut the rail connection to the pier at Lakeside, thereby ensuring that a prime connection to the main rail network had been severed. The Lakeside & Haverthwaite steam railway now runs to link up with the lake steamer service at Lakeside. The steam trains terminate at the left-hand side of this photograph. The original Victorian refreshment and waiting rooms can be seen behind the large steamer.

12 The *Swan* at Bowness around the mid-1960s. Just a few years later in 1971, the scene would change as the modern water buses appeared. Instead of beautifully varnished wood, they were finished in bright colours that included modern materials such as glass fibre, acrylic and formica. *Wynander* of 1971 was followed by *Belle Isle* in 1972 and *Miss Cumbria* in 1974. The influx of new craft gathered pace in following years. These modern water buses may now be classed as being historic as they have been in service for around

13 A scene at Bowness during the 1960s. The strength of steamer services on Windermere during the 1960s compared with Loch Lomond (the largest lake in the UK) is interesting. Windermere, with a somewhat remote location and not being close to any major city, carried more than double the number carried on Loch Lomond. This shows the strength of Windermere as Loch Lomond was close to the sprawling city of Glasgow and, therefore, had a huge potential market. Loch Lomond services were also extensively marketed at the time.

14 A early 1970s scene at Bowness showing three very different lake craft spanning over fifty years. The gigantic *Swan* towers over the small traditional motor boat, while the 1971-built ferry, *Wynander*, is alongside the pier about to board her passengers. The *Wynander* was 40 foot long and could carry up to sixty-four passengers. In the foreground are rowing skiffs that allowed trippers to take a leisurely trip around Bowness Bay.

15 British Rail's maritime division was renamed Sealink and the steamer operation rebranded 'Sealink Windermere' in 1970. In 1984, it was privatised and passed into the ownership of the international shipping conglomerate Sea Containers who renamed it 'The Windermere Iron Steamboat Company', thereby resurrecting a name from the distant past.

16 Perhaps the most unpopular logo ever in the lakes was that of Sealink – the passenger ferry arm of British Rail during the 1970s and 1980s. The somewhat harsh logo of the company (seen here on *Swift*) replaced the older and more attractive name and logo of past Windermere pleasure steamers. In recent years, more attractive and sympathetic logos have been adopted.

17 A pocket timetable for Windermere cruises during the 1975 season. Windermere is the longest lake in the National Park and is 10.5 miles long. It can also become the fastest growing. In a period of a week of heavy rain some 35,700,000,000 litres may be added to the lake. This equates to a rise in the lake of around a metre and a half.
(*J & C McCutcheon Collection*)

SOUVENIR PROGRAMME
OF YOUR CRUISE ON WINDERMERE
WITH POSTCARDS

18 Cover for a souvenir programme containing a guide to cruises on Lake Windermere by the Bowness Bay Boating Company during the 1970s. It included a selection of colour postcards showing the lake and steamers.

19 *Raven* arriving at Glenridding Pier during the 1970s. *Raven* was converted to being a motor ship in 1935, at the same time as her fleet mate. Other changes have been made such as a new funnel and a redesigned saloon. Ultimately though, *Raven* still conjures up the image of a classic Lakeland steamer.

20 The 1930s *Swan* arriving at Bowness around the 1960s. Seath & Company of Glasgow were awarded a contract to build the first *Swan*, a 147-foot, coal-fired, iron-hulled steamer with a capacity of 488 passengers. Launched in 1869, she had a chequered career. In 1893, she sank at her moorings at Lakeside in a gale and a few years later sank again after a collision with *Tern* off of Storrs Hall. Her biggest misfortune occurred on 27 September 1909, when she ran aground at Belle Grange in fog. She was refloated two days later when *Tern* and *Swift*, in tandem, towed her back into the water.

21 Pocket timetable for steamer services on Lake Windermere during the 1979 season. At the time, services were operated by Sealink.

Left: 22 The newly-restored *Western Belle* alongside Glenridding Pier in January 2011.

Below: 23 *Miss Cumbria* entered service on Windermere in 1974. She was built in Holland and was initially transported by sea to Liverpool and then onwards via the M6 to Bowness. *Miss Cumbria* was launched on 16 May 1974.

MISS CUMBRIA — WINDERMERE

24 *Raven* is the largest of the Ullswater steamers and is 112 feet in length, with a width of 15 feet and a gross tonnage of 63 tons. She has a cruising speed of 9–10 knots and can carry up to 246 passengers.

25 *Lady Dorothy* is one of the newer generations of Ullswater steamers. She was built in 1967 and is under half the length of her older Ullswater sisters. She has a gross tonnage of 14 tonnes, a cruising speed of 8 knots and can carry up to 63 passengers. She is ideally suited to cruising during the quieter months of the year.

26 The sedate *Lady of the Lake* and *Lady Dorothy* at Glenridding Pier in 2011. In the foreground is the plaque marking the spot where Donald Campbell launched his boat *Bluebird* in 1955. It was unveiled by his daughter, Gina Campbell, in 1997.

27 The various *Miss Lakeland* vessels offer reliable but basic comfort to around 150 passengers. Each passenger has a seat and has good views of the Windermere shores from the large panoramic windows of the saloon.

28 Motor buses alongside Bowness Pier in early 2011, offering a varied number of lake cruises. Vessels, piers and buildings have been refurbished and updated and the company, through its commitment to sustainable tourism, plays an important part in supporting the local economy. On the hill above the steamer pier you can see the Belsfield Hotel, which was once the home of Mr Henry Schneider – the wealthy industrialist who used to depart regularly from this spot on *Esperance*.

29 The glorious *Gondola* cruising on Coniston during 2007. *Gondola* offers her passengers a wonderful nostalgic glimpse back into the Victorian age of steam in the English Lake District.

30 *Gondola* is the epitome of grand Victorian opulence. Everything about her was designed to attract and entice a prospective passenger.

31 The present *Gondola* is essentially a rebuild to the exact specifications of the original 1859 vessel, and includes some of the original *Gondola*'s fittings. In 1980, she was re-launched again – a hundred and twenty years after her first appearance on Coniston. Today, under the management of the National Trust, she brings delight to countless thousands of twenty-first century passengers.

The *Swift* on Windermere. *Swift* had a long career on the lake and was finally taken out of service in 1981. For a short period, *Swift* became a museum devoted to the speed record history of the Campbell family. She soon deteriorated and despite some attempts to preserve her, she was finally scrapped in 1998, almost 100 years after she was built.
(*J & C McCutcheon Collection*)

In 1961, the season operated between 15 May and 17 September. During that season, the *Swan* and the *Teal* undertook six return sailings a day each, between Lakeside and Ambleside. Additional full runs and intermediate services were offered by the smaller *Swift* and *Tern*. (*Image by Abraham of Keswick*)

Bunting is flying as *Teal* experiences her finest moment in August 1956, when she carried Her Majesty Queen Elizabeth II and the Duke of Edinburgh on a cruise from Ambleside to Bowness. A signed photograph was later placed on the steamer to mark this special visit. This view shows the Queen and Prince Phillip standing under the bridge and about to disembark at Bowness Pier. (*J & C McCutcheon Collection*)

The Teal' Lake Windermere   S.224

Most people agree that there are sixteen lakes in the Lake District. There is also many other areas of water called 'tarns'. Although some tarns are bigger than so called lakes, most of the tarns are very small and some don't even have names. The Lake District is England's largest National Park and covers an area of 885 square miles. There is only one official lake – Bassenthwaite Lake. All of the others are 'waters' or 'meres'. This image of *Teal* shows the majesty of the Lakeland mountains. (*J & C McCutcheon Collection*)

Windermere Lake. 5127

In 1947, there was a fuel shortage, which resulted in the coal-fired steamers on Windermere not entering service. This meant that *Teal* and *Swan* were joined by the *Cygnet*. Here, one of the large steamers is seen with one of the traditional small launches in the foreground disembarking passengers at one of the smaller landing points around the lake. (*J & C McCutcheon Collection*)

A rare view showing the two propellers of the *Swan* while on the slipway at Lakeside, photographed around 1965. Paddle steamers only had a limited life in service on Windermere and propellers soon became the predominant form of propulsion. (*J & C McCutcheon Collection*)

The engine of the *Tern* was removed and stored at Lakeside on 29 December 1957. *Tern* was originally built with large and slow moving propellers. This gave her a particularly smooth and gliding movement on the lake. In 1958, she was rebuilt with two Gleniffer diesel engines, capable of providing a speed of 12 mph. (*J & C McCutcheon Collection*)

The Engine Room of the *Swift* pictured around 1958. Originally, she had four-cylinder steam engines made by Fisher of Paisley. These were replaced with the two Gleniffer diesel engines shown here in 1956, after they became troublesome. (*J & C McCutcheon Collection*)

The engine from the Windermere steamer *Tern* was removed and stored at Lakeside Station on 29 December 1957. The original steam engine was quite unique as it used a boiler of locomotive-type design with two firebox doors, one on either side of the ship towards the front of the boiler room. (*J & C McCutcheon Collection*)

Tern re-entered service on 18 May 1958, with new engines and a new funnel. At the same time, her fine saloons were also redecorated. Her first-class saloon, towards the bow, was refurbished with curtains, carpets, fabric and décor in a rich, dark wine-red colour. Similarly, the walls of this saloon were finished in white with decorative features picked out in gold. (*J & C McCutcheon Collection*)

The upper deck of *Swan* while cruising on Windermere during the 1950s. *Swan* is showing her original uncovered deck complete with varnished wooden seats. The previous *Swan* was a well-loved steamer on Windermere. But by the 1930s, she had become far too small. Her owners, the mighty London, Midland & Scottish Railway, placed an order for this new, sleek and far larger *Swan*. The gallant and elegant old *Swan*, therefore, ended her days in the scrap yard after sixty-nine years of service. (*J & C McCutcheon Collection*)

The *Swan* at Bowness Pier. By 1968, the cost of a first-class, full-lake cruise ticket was ten shillings. At the time, both first- and second-class fares were offered with second class being around 25 per cent cheaper. The timetable notes that a first-class, seven-day season ticket cost thirty shillings and that 'tobacco and light refreshments' were available aboard the *Swan* and *Teal*.

A central influence to the steamers on Lake Windermere has always been that of the railways. From the initial heavy involvement of the Furness Railway to the 1923 amalgamation of the 'Big Four', when the London, Midland & Scottish Railway reigned supreme, things have rarely changed. This was carried on into the post-war nationalisation of the railways and Sealink. From all of these quite major changes of ownership, little has happened to the little lake-steamer fleet.

The change in holiday habits that affected the rest of the UK had limited effects on the Lake Windermere steamers. People in the 1960s were now going abroad for cheap foreign holidays and the motor car was becoming pre-eminent, but people still flocked to the Lake District. Yes, there were changes to reflect the changing needs of passengers such as more covered passenger accommodation and steamers were withdrawn, but all in all things changed very little. This may be linked to the fact that the steamers were of a size that made them relatively economic and they also cruised on a freshwater lake. (*J & C McCutcheon Collection*)

In the twenty-seven years between 1937 and 1964, passenger numbers on Windermere changed very little. In 1937, 492,500 passengers were carried. By the mid-1950s, over 453,240 were carried. A year later in 1956, over 400,000 passengers were carried, but this was broken in 1964 when over half a million were carried around the lake.

Teal departing from Lakeside. During the 1964 season, steamer services on Windermere operated between 11 May and 20 September, showing how much the season was catering for the summer tourist traffic. This was, of course, during the times when the three large steamers were operating.

LOVELY WINDERMERE

SAILINGS BY m.v. SWAN m.v. TEAL m.v. SWIFT m.v. TERN

British Railways
LONDON MIDLAND REGION   *SUMMER 1965*

AMBLESIDE At the northern end of the lake and close by the meeting of those delightful streams Rothay and Brathay, Ambleside is a delightful town, reasonably unspoilt.

Approaching it by water—and this is undoubtedly quite the most rewarding way of coming to Ambleside—one enjoys wonderful views of Wansfell, Loughrigg, the Langdale Pikes and the Scafell Range as well as many other Lakeland peaks. The mountain scenery at the head of the lake is most impressive. Ambleside is an excellent centre for exploring Southern Lakeland and among the nearer attractions are Grasmere, Rydal, Langdale, the lovely Rothay valley and Stock Ghyll waterfalls. One of the sights of Ambleside itself is the curious little Bridge House, now used as a National Trust information centre.

BOWNESS AND WINDERMERE Midway along the eastern shore of the lake, beautifully situated opposite the lovely Belle Isle, Bowness and its close neighbour, Windermere Town, are one of the main tourist centres of the Lake District.

Orrest Head, just to the north of Windermere, is a noted vantage point from which superb views of the surrounding country can be obtained.

Lake Windermere's scenery is vividly contrasted and Bowness marks the transition from the colourful fells and wooded shores of the lower reaches to the spectacular ruggedness around its headwaters.

LAKE SIDE is the starting point for the motor vessels which ply between Lake Side, Bowness and Ambleside. Lake Side is set in pleasant scenery at the foot of the lake but greater pleasure is in the anticipation of the enjoyment which lies ahead as you embark.

A 1965 brochure for cruises on Windermere. Windermere was advertised as the 'Queen of the Lakes'. At the time, one vessel a day was offered solely for the use of party groups between 1 May to 4 July, and 30 August and 19 September. Groups of ten or more were given reduced fares. Road–rail–ship combined tours were also offered.

Swift at Bowness in around the 1950s. *Swift* suffered boiler problems in 1956 and was taken out of service. The following year she re-entered service with new oil engines as well as a new funnel. The company were pleased with this work and during the following year *Tern* was converted in a similar fashion. Throughout the years, there has been an emphasis on converting Lake District steamers rather than ordering new tonnage. This has meant that the steamers have had long and successful lives.

Teal departing from Lakeside. The Lakeside pier was an immediate success after its completion in 1869. It offered steamers more than adequate deep-water facilities. This in turn led to wider development of the steamer fleet to include larger and better iron-hulled steamers. The branch railway line from Ulverston to Lakeside closed on 5 September 1965, leaving the Windermere steamers without a direct mainline rail link. Luckily, a group of volunteers raised enough money to reopen the line from Haverthwaite to Lakeside some years later. This now thrives as a preserved steam railway for visitors. (*J & C McCutcheon Collection*)

lovely
windermere

SAILINGS BY
m.v. **SWAN**   m.v. **TEAL**
m.v. **SWIFT**   m.v. **TERN**

British Rail | London Midland Region

SUMMER 1968

Right: A brochure outlining services by the *Swan*, *Teal*, *Tern* and *Swift* during the summer of 1968. At the time, a two-class service was still offered to passengers. The price of a full cruise between Lakeside and Ambleside was 50p if you travelled first class with a 25 per cent reduction for second class. Light refreshments were offered on the *Swan* and *Teal*.

Opposite above: During the 1950s, British Rail ran regular excursions including one from many towns and cities in the north and midlands to the Lakes. For instance, they offered an excursion from Birmingham on summer weekends for £1 per adult return. Passengers joined the train in the morning for a trip to Windermere Town Station, where they were allowed time for sightseeing and shopping before boarding the steamer at Bowness Pier for a cruise via Ambleside before boarding their return train at Lakeside. They arrived back in Birmingham at 1.00 a.m. the following morning. (*J & C McCutcheon Collection*)

Opposite below: Swan on the way to Lakeside around the 1950s. Note that passenger and crew comfort has changed from earlier photographs. Her open-top deck now has canvas dodgers around the sides as well as an awning for use during wet and cold weather. Likewise, the bridge is now made of wood and has been enclosed. Lakeside was the original hub of the Windermere steamer service and still remains crucial to the success of services on the lake. Nowadays, the Lakeside & Haverthwaite Railway provides an excellent preserved tourist link, enabling passengers to connect up with the steamers. New attractions have also grown up, such as the Lakes Aquarium to provide an extra attraction. Cafes and a shop complete the facilities at Lakeside. During the winter months, the older and larger steamers are repaired on the adjacent slipway. (*J & C McCutcheon Collection*)

The ferry services on Windermere and Ullswater are now more or less the sole survivors of the many passenger ferry services that once plied the north-west coast of the UK. These now lost services disappeared because of competition, new roads and rail links as well as changing tastes. The surviving services in England's Lakeland now provide the main link back to earlier times. (*J & C McCutcheon Collection*)

A somewhat bland pocket timetable listing services on Windermere during the 1969 season. The special 'Three Pier Ticket' gave passengers a 21-mile-long cruise lasting some two and a half hours. Passengers were allowed to break their journey with time on shore at Bowness, Ambleside and Lakeside.

The 1938-built *Swan* on Windermere. In 1869, the first screw steamer named *Swan* came into service on the lake. She entered service at the time when the Lakeside branch was opened by the Furness Railway.

Lake Windermere was always the most dominant lake for pleasure steamers. It had access to two railway links at Windermere and Lakeside stations as well as being the largest lake in England. In addition, it had early ferry links as people around its shores needed transportation. It remains today the busiest lake for steamer cruises.

A scene at Bowness in the 1960s. In 1964, the number of passengers carried aboard the Windermere steamers exceeded 500,000. This was only for the second time in the service's history. In the following year, only three ships operated the service outside of the peak summer season of 5 July to 29 August. This left one vessel free to undertake charter work.

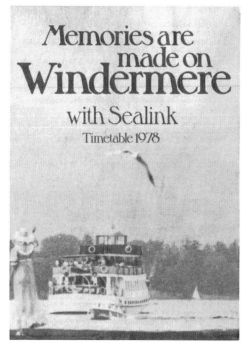

Pocket timetable for steamer services on Windermere operated by Sealink during the 1978 season. The main season ran between 30 April and 1 October of that year. The timetable gives full details of the linked service of the Lakeside & Haverthwaite Railway.

It's a wonderful Windermere day
THE HYDRO LAKELINER DAY

Lake Sail-n-Luncheon

A superb luncheon at the
3-star Hydro Hotel, Bowness,
and a cruise on one of Sealink's
Lake Liners – all for an inclusive
price of just

£2·75

incl. VAT (at 8%) &
service charge

Sealink WINDERMERE

Lake District steamers have always tried different initiatives to attract new business. The coach-tour market has always been an important one. This leaflet from 1979 offered coach passengers a three-course lunch of soup, roast chicken and sherry trifle at the Hydro Hotel above Bowness Pier, along with a lake cruise for the inclusive price of £2.75.

The *Teal* cruising during her heyday. Many people will be surprised by the fact that the English Lake District has perhaps the largest concentration of pleasure steamers in the UK. Perhaps the only other areas to beat Cumbria are London, the River Thames and Devon. (*J & C McCutcheon Collection*)

Some of the traditional, highly-varnished, wooden-hulled steamers at Bowness during post-war years. These small pleasure boats offered a more intimate, varied and comfortable cruise experience. Alongside these, a flotilla of rowing skiffs can be seen, which were hired by holidaymakers. The ticket office and the Belsfield Hotel can be seen in the distance.

The majority of steam launches were relatively small, with most measuring between 15 feet and up to 55 in length. Many were elaborate picnic boats and their wealthy passengers paraded in full view of their neighbours. Eating and drinking was a grand Victorian tradition and these steamers were the perfect canvas to display the feast of tea and scones. Even the tea was prepared in a 'Windermere kettle', where a coil from the boiler quickly heated water in a highly-polished copper urn. Other yachts were used for fishing for char as well as ferrying people around the lake to church and to visit friends. Some even had sleeping accommodation and toilets.
(*J & C McCutcheon Collection*)

The era of steam yachts on Windermere reached its peak in the latter part of the nineteenth century, although sailing yachts were used for a long time before that. The Windermere steam yachts were grand and stylish statements of the wealth and position of their owners and they evolved a more or less unique style in the UK. Many of these were preserved in the Windermere Steamboat Museum at Bowness during the 1970s. (*J & C McCutcheon Collection*)

Teal at Lakeside Pier in 2004. Pleasure boat cruises are as popular as ever in the Lake District. In 2000 alone, over 1.2 million passengers were carried on the lake steamers. Further investment at the time in passenger facilities gave steamer services a facelift. On Ullswater at Glenridding, a new purpose-built booking office, café and shop was built, and similarly on Windermere at Lakeside, a new Lake District aquarium was opened alongside the old Victorian steamer pier adjacent to the Lakeside & Haverthwaite Railway.

Miss Lakeland alongside the pier at Bowness in January 2011. The day-tripper is the lifeblood of the service on Windermere. Today, the vast majority of passengers arrive by car or coach, but the rail connection at Windermere remains and a portion of the old Lakeside branch prospers as a preserved steam railway. Bowness is situated approximately a mile from the town of Windermere with its railway station.

Miss Westmoreland arriving at Bowness in February 2011. Vessels like *Miss Westmoreland* are cheap to operate and offer a year-round service for passengers. During the summer months, they operate on the shorter routes and tours around the lake.

Teal departing from Bowness during her early career. In May 1993, the Windermere company amalgamated with the Bowness Bay Boating Company. This enabled historic steamers to sail alongside atmospheric launches such as *Queen of the Lake*. The company now operates under the name of 'Windermere Lake Cruises'. Since the merger, a considerable amount of money has been spent on improving every aspect of steamer operation.

Swan at Bowness Pier. The 1960s to 1980s witnessed the introduction of the water buses, further structural alterations to the *Swan* and *Teal*, as well as changes in ownership. The start of the twenty-first century showed the Windermere lake steamers to be in an excellent position. They had a perfectly balanced mix of the old with the new, thereby keeping alive the style and romance of the Victorian and 1930s eras, along with a timetable and marketing strategy that reflects the needs of a now year-round clientele.

A souvenir china dish from the 1950s showing the well-loved *Swan* on Windermere. Souvenirs have always been sold aboard the Lake District steamers. The most popular gifts have included enamelled badges, china and countless postcards.

Teal alongside Bowness Pier during her LMS days. The lakeside buildings at Bowness haven't changed over the years. They still offer refreshments as well as ticket facilities, as they did when they were built.

Swan at Waterhead during the late 1950s. Waterhead has remained the least busy of the three principle Windermere piers due to it having no rail link.

From Waterhead (Ambleside) to Lakeside, the lake is 10.5 miles long and is one mile across at its widest point. The greatest depth is 219 feet. It is a freshwater lake leading out from Lakeside through the un-navigable River Leven into the sea at Morecambe Bay.

Teal having just left Waterhead. Ambleside has changed little since Victorian times, when the buildings in Lake Road, Rothay Road and Church Street were built to cater for the huge expansion in the tourism industry. The unique quality of the Lake District has been preserved through the creation of the Lake District National Park. Little has been achieved to deal with the growth of motor traffic. Today, older industries in woodlands, mines and quarries has virtually disappeared. Tourism and its controlled building development has become the only major area of enterprise and employment. The Windermere lake steamers remain virtually unaffected by these changes.

The large Windermere steamers *Swan*, *Teal* and *Tern*, along with the water buses, continue to operate the main service between Lakeside, Bowness and Ambleside, as well as standard tours. Smaller and traditional lake steamers carrying around thirty to fifty passengers operate on Windermere. These run to places such as the Brockhole – the home of the National Park Centre. There are plans to build a new large pier at the side of the lake to allow the large steamers to call and to allow passengers to find out more about the Lake District National Park through displays and events at the centre.

WINDERMERE LAKE CRUISES

Prices and timing are subject to alteration without notice

1987 TIMETABLES

Season: Friday 17th April – Sunday 4th October

"MAGICAL MINI CRUISES"

Round trip from Bowness Pier (45 minutes) Daily except Saturday

| Dep: | 10.45 | 11.45 | 12.45 | 13.45 | 14.45 | 15.45 | 16.45 |
| Arr: | 11.30 | 12.30 | 13.30 | 14.30 | 15.30 | 16.30 | 17.30 |

"ALONG THE LAKE CRUISES"

Daily from Lakeside

Lakeside – Bowness 35 minutes
| Dep: | 09.15 | 11.15 | 12.15 | 14.15 | 15.15 | 17.15 |
| Arr: | 09.50 | 11.50 | 12.50 | 14.50 | 15.50 | 17.50 |

Lakeside – Ambleside 1½ hours
| Dep: | 09.15 | 11.15 | 12.15 | 14.15 | 15.15 | 17.15(NS) |
| Arr: | 10.40 | 12.40 | 13.40 | 15.40 | 16.40 | 18.40* |

Daily from Bowness

Bowness – Ambleside 30 minutes
| Dep: | 10.10 | 12.10 | 13.10 | 15.10 | 16.10 | 17.25 | 18.10(NS) |
| Arr: | 10.40 | 12.40 | 13.40 | 15.40 | 16.40 | 17.50 | 18.40 |

Bowness – Lakeside 35 minutes
| Dep: | 10.25 | 11.25 | 13.25 | 14.25 | 16.25 | 18.00 | 19.20(F) |
| Arr: | 11.00 | 12.00 | 14.00 | 15.00 | 17.00 | 18.35 | 19.55 |

Daily from Ambleside

Ambleside – Bowness 30 minutes
| Dep: | 09.50 | 10.50 | 12.50 | 13.50 | 15.50 | 16.50 | 18.50(NS) |
| Arr: | 10.15 | 11.15 | 13.15 | 14.15 | 16.15 | 17.15 | 19.15 |

Ambleside – Lakeside 1½ hours
| Dep: | 09.50 | 10.50 | 12.50 | 13.50 | 15.50 | 18.50(F) |
| Arr: | 11.00 | 12.00 | 14.00 | 15.00 | 17.00 | 19.55 |

*Change at Bowness (NS) Not Saturdays (F) Fridays only
Vessels also available for private hire/charter by special arrangement after October 4th.

Ten Miles of Magic!!

For further information
and brochures please contact:-

**Windermere Iron Steamboat Co. Ltd.,
Lakeside, Ulverston, Cumbria LA12 8AS.
Tel: Newby Bridge (05395) 31188.**

Don't miss the boat, send for Great Ideas for Groups

1) Windermere Day — Steamtrain/Cruise on Lake/Brockhole National Park Centre. ☐
2) Lakeside Hotel's Steamsail — Steamtrain/Lunch at Lakeside Hotel/Cruise on Lake. ☐
3) Waterhead Sailscene or Royal Sailscene — Lunch/High Tea at Hotel/Cruise on Lake. ☐
4) Lakeland Heritage Day — Steamtrain/Cruise on Lake/Steamboat Museum. ☐
5) The Hydro Lakeliner — Lunch/High Tea at Hotel/Cruise on Lake. ☐
6) Charter of Vessel — Works Outings/Weddings, etc. ☐
7) Panoramic Lakeland — Visit Cartmel/Grasmere/Cruise on Lake/Brockhole. ☐

Tick Box and Return to:-

**Windermere Iron Steamboat Co. Ltd.,
Lakeside, Ulverston, Cumbria LA12 8AS.
Tel: Newby Bridge (05395) 31188.**

FARES

Children under 5 travel free. Children between 5 and 16 travel at half price.

"MAGICAL MINI CRUISE" £2.00 per person

"ALONG THE LAKE CRUISES"

	Single	Return	Family Tickets	
Lakeside – Bowness (or vice versa)	£1.50 per person	£3.00 per person	(Up to 2 adults and 3 children,	
Bowness – Ambleside (or vice versa)	£1.50 per person	£3.00 per person	5 and under 16 years)	
Lakeside – Ambleside (or vice versa)	£3.00 per person	£5.00 per person	Freedom of the Lake	£12.50
Round the Lake		£5.00 per person		
3 Day Holiday Ticket		£9.00 per person	Bowness and Ambleside Sail	£7.75
7 Day Holiday Ticket		£14.00 per person	Bowness and Lakeside Sail	£7.75

Group Fares are available on request from Windermere Iron Steamboat Company

Prices and timings are subject to change without notice.

WINDERMERE LAKE CRUISES AND THE LAKESIDE AND HAVERTHWAITE RAILWAY

	Single	Return	Family Tickets	
Haverthwaite – Bowness	£2.40	£4.40	(Up to 2 adults and 3 children,	
Children (5 and under 16)	£1.40	£2.25	5 and under 16 years)	
Haverthwaite – Ambleside	£3.75	£6.20	Freedom of the Lake and Railway	£16.15
Children (5 and under 16)	£2.06	£3.15	Haverthwaite Bowness Rail and Sail	£12.00
Children under 5 free			We reserve the right to cancel sailings during severe weather conditions	

Pocket timetable for Windermere cruises offered by the Iron Steamboat Company during the 1987 season. At the time, a full return between Lakeside and Ambleside cost £5. The main summer timetable ran between 17 April and 4 October. Outside of that time, vessels were available for charter work.

Miss Cumbria II at Bowness in 2010. The large pier at Bowness indicates how important the calling point was to steamer services. Vessels like *Miss Cumbria II* have allowed the service to flourish on Windermere by offering more cost-effective cruise services.

The newer water-bus vessels may not have the grace and lines of the Victorian steamers, but they offer covered accommodation for twelve months of the year.

A splendid view of *Swan* departing from Bowness during the 1960s. This view provides a link back to the earliest days of Windermere lake steamers. The Furness Railway built a splendid fleet of steamers that remained firm favourites for generations of Lake Windermere trippers. Names such as *Tern*, *Swift*, *Cygnet* and *Swan* had long and busy lives. Some were replaced during the LMS days by the larger *Swan* and *Teal* during the mid-1930s. Changes in the 1970s resulted in newer water buses. What makes the Windermere fleet stand out from most pleasure boat areas of the UK is the fact that it has seen few changes during the past century and a half. It continues to have a nostalgic appeal for generation after generation of Lake District holidaymakers, offering historic and atmospheric steamers with twenty-first-century facilities and marketing.

3

Ullswater Steamers

Ullswater is one of the most spectacular lakes of the English Lake District. It is quite unique in that two steamers, *Raven* and *Lady of the Lake*, have cruised on Ullswater for well over one hundred years.

A steamer on Ullswater viewed from Martindale Hause. *Lady of the Lake* was launched on 26 June 1877. She had been designed by Douglas Hebson of Penrith, but was built in Glasgow. She was transported the 120 miles from Glasgow to Penrith in three sections by rail and then from Penrith by horse carts to Waterside near Pooley Bridge, where she was finally assembled. *Lady of the Lake* is 110 feet in length, with a width of 15 feet and a gross tonnage of 43 tons. Her cruising speed is 10 knots and she can carry up to 220 passengers. (*J & C McCutcheon Collection*)

Raven was originally launched on 11 July 1889 for service on Ullswater. Her builders were the same as for the *Lady of the Lake*. *Raven* was named after a house on the shores of Ullswater named Ravencragg. She was the largest steamer built for service on Ullswater.

The pier at Howtown with a steamer approaching. The pier is situated under the shadow of Hallin Fell with Gowbarrow visible in the distance. The Ullswater Steam Navigation Company was formed in 1855 to run steamer services on the lake. (*J & C McCutcheon Collection*)

Services on Ullswater started in 1849 with the start of services between Pooley Bridge and Patterdale. The Ullswater steamers, during their early years, always had a role in transporting mail, goods and locals around the lake. The *Enterprise*, a paddle steamer, was launched on 13 August 1859 for service on Ullswater. Little is known of her, but it is thought that she sank somewhere on the lake.

3014. The "Raven" Leaving Pooley Bridge. Ullswater

Raven departing from Pooley Bridge Pier on Ullswater. When *Raven* entered service the *Cumberland and Westmoreland Gazette* stated that 'it is questionable if there be any boat to beat, or even equal this little craft on any lake in this country'.

An idyllic view of Pooley Bridge Pier showing a steamer alongside the pier. Pooley Bridge is positioned at the northern end of Ullswater. The village was once a busy market town, specialising in fish in the days before Penrith became prominent. The village has since catered for the tourist industry, with many of its visitors arriving aboard an Ullswater steamer.

A view of Pooley Bridge Pier and pier house around 1905. A steamer can be seen alongside the pier and passengers are transferring to horse coach and motor car to continue their sightseeing. Pooley Bridge and Glenridding are the largest and most important settlements on Ullswater. Originally, the lake steamers would have helped the villages with transferring goods, livestock and local villagers. Today, the local economy is almost entirely concentrated on catering for tourists, with around 90 per cent of visitors arriving by car.
(*J & C McCutcheon Collection*)

4026. ULLSWATER HOTEL FROM THE LAKE.

The Ullswater Hotel (now the Inn on the Lake) is the close neighbour to the pier and facilities at Glenridding. Here, *Raven* is departing on a cruise. Note the original tall and slender funnel and lack of enclosed wheelhouse that gave *Raven* a graceful if somewhat exposed feel.

Opposite below: Raven's original steam machinery was replaced by two eight-cylinder oil engines in 1935. These were built by the National Gas Seven Oil Engine Company of Ashton-under-Lyme. Her funnel was changed to a larger motor-ship one at the same time. *Raven*'s bridge was originally behind her funnel and her engines were replaced by Thorneycroft in 1964. At around the same time, her bridge was moved further forwards to the front of the saloon. This quite dramatically altered her original look.

Above: Howtown Bay with the steamer pier. Ullswater is the second largest lake in the Lake District. It has a length of 7.5 miles, with a depth in places of 205 feet. It is sometimes called the 'Dark Lake' and several hundreds of years ago it was thought to be inhabited by monsters. Howtown is positioned on the eastern shore of Ullswater around halfway up the length of the lake, three and a half miles from Pooley Bridge.

Raven approaching Howtown Pier around 1910. In 1895, *Raven* was transformed into a temporary royal yacht when her decks were painted yellow to mark the visit of the German Kaiser Wilhelm II to Lowther Castle, which was owned by Lord Lonsdale. (*Image by Abraham of Keswick*)

The *Raven* arriving at Patterdale during the early part of her career. Note the open bridge on the steamer. The Second World War witnessed many new water-based users of Ullswater; the lake was used to train servicemen. They were instructed in how to use flying boats, mini submarines and other small naval craft. *Lady of the Lake* and *Raven* also carried servicemen for training at the Ullswater Hotel at Glenridding. (*Image by Abraham of Keswick*)

A steamer arriving at Howtown in around 1900. In April 1802, William Wordsworth was inspired to write the famous poem 'Daffodils' after seeing daffodils growing on the shores of Ullswater on a journey back to Grasmere. Wordsworth once wrote of Ullswater: 'it is the happiest combination of beauty and grandeur, which any of the lakes affords'.

Raven embarking her passengers at Pooley Bridge around 1928. Glenridding is the main pier on Ullswater with Pooley Bridge and Howtown being smaller. The freshwater lakes of the Lake District has ensured that steamers such as the *Lady of the Lake* have survived longer than their seawater cousins.

232 Steamer arriving at Glenridding Ullswater.

Lady of the Lake arriving at Glenridding Pier on Ullswater. *Lady of the Lake* was originally used as a Royal Mail steamer. She also provided a quick and reliable ferry service to people living around the shores of the lake in the days before the motor car. The *Lady of the Lake*'s four-cylinder steam engine was replaced by two Crossley diesels in 1935. At around that time she received her large motor-ship funnel. This was frowned upon by many people. At this time the saloon had been shortened again to just eight windows, as can be seen in this image. (*Image by Abraham of Keswick*)

An aerial view showing Pooley Bridge Pier. Ullswater may not be the most well-known and popular lake in the Lake District, but it makes up for this in its beauty.

A steamer departing from Pooley Bridge in around 1950. Note the larger funnel that replaced the tall thin one during the 1930s. On 25 January 1966, *Lady of the Lake* was damaged by fire after an explosion in a nearby hut where spare engine parts were stored for the *Raven*. Damage was estimated at £2,000.

The full beauty of Ullswater can be appreciated in this image of *Lady of the Lake* cruising amid stunning scenery. *Lady of the Lake* is believed to be the oldest working passenger vessel in the world. Many reckon that Ullswater as the most beautiful of the English lakes and it has been compared to Lake Lucerne in Switzerland. It is a typical Lake District narrow 'ribbon lake' with the surrounding mountains giving Ullswater the shape of an elongated 'Z', giving it three separate reaches that weave their way through the surrounding hills.

Bluebird broke the world speed record on Ullswater along with Sir Donald Campbell in July 1955, when a speed of 202.32 mph was recorded – a speed somewhat exaggerated from *Raven* and *Lady of the Lake*. A launching site and boat house was provided adjacent to Glenridding Pier. This was supplied by Lord Wakefield, whose engineering company built *Bluebird K7* at Preston.

The *Raven* departing from Pooley Bridge during the mid-1930s. This was the time when *Raven* was converted. The length of the queue on the steamer and crowded decks indicate that this was the height of the tourist season.

Ullswater is the second largest lake in the Lake District. The lake provides the natural boundary between the old counties of Cumberland and Westmoreland. It has a maximum depth of around 60 metres.

Raven at the head of Ullswater during the late 1950s. Note the amount of open deck space, which was excellent in good weather. In more recent times, a lot of the deck space has been covered with awnings to protect passengers from the elements. The *Raven* can now carry up to 246 passengers and although younger, gives a similar heritage appearance to the *Lady of the Lake*.

Raven has had a luckier history than the *Lady of the Lake*, with no major disasters affecting her. The Lakes have witnessed the sinking of many steamers. The *Lady of the Lake*, for example, has had a career marked by a number of dramatic and negative experiences.

Ship enthusiasts generally hotly debate any changes to a steamer and the Lake District was no different to other areas. This happened when the *Lady of the Lake* had her original and traditional stove-pipe funnel replaced in around 1935 with a shorter more modern one.

Lady of the Lake has had a chequered history. In 1881, she sank at her moorings and was later refloated by a team of divers. Bad luck struck again when she sank in 1958 during a terrible storm. Seven years later, she was badly damaged by a fire and didn't return to service for another fourteen years. She was re-launched by William Whitelaw MP – the Deputy Prime Minister – on 19 May 1979.

A CRUISE ON

ULLSWATER

for an ideal outing on— **M.Y. "RAVEN" or "LADY OF THE LAKE"**
FULLY LICENSED

SPECIAL TERMS QUOTED FOR HIRE OF MOTOR YACHT FOR ORGANISED PARTIES

NIGHT CRUISES AND DANCES ARRANGED

TIME TABLE 1980

30th March to
7th November

Sundays included

Service C does not
operate after
30th September

SERVICE		A	B	C
Glenridding	Dep.	11-30	2-00	4-30
Howtown	Dep.	12-05	2-35	5-05
Pooley Bridge	Arr.	12-25	2-55	5-25
Pooley Bridge	Dep.	12-45	3-15	5-30
Howtown	Dep.	1-05	3-35	5-50
Glenridding	Arr.	1-40	4-10	6-25

Fares between   under 14
Pooley Bridge and Howtown   60p.   60p.
Pooley Bridge and Glenridding   £1.10   85p.
Glenridding and Howtown   75p.   75p.
Round the Lake Special Fare   £1.80   £1.30
Round the Lake Family Ticket
(2 adults and 4 children)   £6-00

*Services and Fares may be altered without notice. Services will be
adhered to weather permitting.*
*The contract and liability of the Company are limited exclusively to
their own yachts. For further information and details apply to :—*
Ullswater Navigation & Transit Co. Ltd., *13, Maude Street, Kendal.*
Tel. 21626

Merritt's, Printers, Windermere

Handbill advertising cruises on Ullswater during the 1980 season. The timetable ran from
30 March to 7 November during that year and a ticket for a full cruise cost £1.80.

The steamer service on Ullswater is now a year-round service. *Raven* and *Lady of the Lake* have been adapted to fulfil this new role admirably. They now offer an excellent mixture of covered and heated-passenger accommodation along with open deck space for good weather. Tourism in the Lakes is now a year-round phenomenon with tourists taking short breaks in the winter and times such as Christmas, when the Lakes are often at their best.

Raven at Glenridding. The Windermere-based *Cygnet* of 1879 was purchased in the 1950s for future operations on Ullswater. She was then painted in the Ullswater-steamer colours in readiness for the transfer. By 1961, she was deteriorating badly at Lakeside after being found to be too large to transport by the existing roads. By 1962, *Cygnet* had sunk with only her funnel and mast visible above the water. She had also suffered from vandalism.

Raven alongside Pooley Bridge Pier during the 1966 summer season. During the 1971 season, *Raven* was in service between May and September. She operated three-round trips a day between Glenridding, Howtown and Pooley Bridge. The cost of the return fare was 37.5p. (*J & C McCutcheon Collection*)

In 1961, Manchester Corporation promoted a Parliamentary Bill to turn Ullswater into a reservoir. In 1962, Lord Birkett defeated the Bill in the House of Lords. He died the following day and had stopped an environmental disaster.

Pooley Bridge Pier was badly damaged in the floods of 2009. It was rebuilt extensively in 2010 to allow full passenger use. Great care was taken during the rebuild to ensure that the fragile ecology of Ullswater wasn't disturbed. Particular care was taken to ensure that the spawning grounds of the Atlantic salmon weren't disturbed.

Keeping a fleet of historic steamers operating is an expensive and time-consuming business. Here, the *Raven* is seen heavily clad in scaffolding and covers to ensure good-working conditions during 2011. As well as work to the hull and saloons of the steamer, the Maritime & Coastguard Agency also need to inspect the hull each year.

Lady Dorothy and *Lady of the Lake* at Glenridding. Ullswater never gained the popularity of Windermere mainly because of the poor access of the railway to the lake. The Ullswater steamers probably owe their longevity to the somewhat unchanging business of passenger traffic on Ullswater, unlike Windermere. On the lake, the 1930s built *Swan* and *Teal* were built to accommodate a greater influx of visitors from the 1930s onwards.

The bow and nameboard of the *Lady of the Lake* at Glenridding. *Lady of the Lake* can now carry up to 220 passengers.

A winter scene at Glenridding in 2011. Glenridding is used to moor most of the Ullswater fleet during the winter months. On the left is the *Lady Dorothy* with *Lady of the Lake* on the right-hand side. The *Western Belle* was also moored at Glenridding at this time while *Lady Wakefield* was at Pooley Bridge. *Raven* was undergoing repairs on the slipway.

A view at Glenridding Pier in 2011. Glenridding is the largest village on the shores of Ullswater and is the principle calling point of the Ullswater lake steamers. It contrasts greatly with the huge steamer piers at Bowness and Lakeside on Windermere.

Lady of the Lake at Glenridding in 2011. During the autumn of 1963, two MP's appealed at a planning enquiry in June to seek a reversal of the Lake District Planning Board's decision to turn down an application for a pier to be built on the western shores of the lake. It was announced that the *Lady of the Lake* and *Raven* had lost about £1,000 a year during the previous five years. The deficit had been made up out of the pockets of directors. It was thought that a new pier might reverse the situation and permission was given for a temporary floating jetty to be positioned at Aird Green as an experiment for three years.

Lady of the Lake and *Lady Dorothy* at Glenridding in 2011.

The old and the new – *Lady Dorothy* (foreground) and *Lady of the Lake* alongside Glenridding Pier in 2011.

Lady Wakefield at Pooley Bridge in February 2011. *Berry Castle* (now *Lady Wakefield*) was sold during the early 1970s as the fortunes of her owners, River Dart Steamboat Company, declined. Apart from returning to River Dart service, she saw further service on the River Medway in Kent (as *Golden Cormorant*) close to another native vessel of the River Dart – the operational paddle-steamer *Kingswear Castle*.

Lady Wakefield at Pooley Bridge in January 2011. *Lady Wakefield* was built in 1949 and is 67 feet in length and has a width of 16.5 feet. Her gross tonnage is 45 tonnes. She has a cruising speed of 9 knots and can carry up to 150 passengers.

Lady Dorothy during a cruise in January 2011. The acquisition of *Lady Dorothy* in 2001 meant that for the first time a winter service could be operated on Ullswater. This catered for the growing number of tourists and walkers visiting the Lake District during winter months. On many cruises, most passengers enjoy the warmth of the cosy saloon, while some hardy walkers enjoy the winter sunshine and breathtaking scenery on deck.

A view from the stern of the *Lady Dorothy* en route between Glenridding and Pooley Bridge in 2011. The Kirkstone Pass can be seen in the far distance. It is the Lake District's highest pass with an altitude of 1,489 feet. It links the two largest steamer services of the Lake District with Glenridding at one end and Ambleside on Windermere at the other.

Lady Wakefield was renamed by HRH Princess Alexandra at a ceremony in April 2007, after conversion for service on Ullswater. She was built in 1949 by Philip of Dartmouth (the builder of the coal-fired, paddle-steamer *Kingswear Castle*).

The newest Ullswater steamer was the *Western Belle*. She was originally launched on Saturday 30 November 1935 by Molly Thorne, the youngest daughter of the manager of the yard that built her. She was 69.9 feet long, 15.3 feet wide and 5.4 feet deep and could carry up to 283 passengers.

Western Belle was built for service on the River Tamar from Plymouth to Millbrook for the Millbrook Steam Boat & Trading Company by Fellows of Great Yarmouth in 1935. She was a replacement for the *Whitsand Castle*. She was at times used for Plymouth Dockyard cruises.

The latest addition to the fast expanding Ullswater fleet was the *Western Belle* in 2008. This boat had originally operated at Plymouth and on the River Thames. After arriving on Ullswater, a lengthy and sympathetic restoration and conversion took place to ensure that the steamer complimented the quality of the other steamers of the Ullswater fleet. She is pictured here at Glenridding in 2011. *Western Belle* undertook the long and dangerous delivery journey from the Thames by sea to Maryport in July 2008. The main part of her restoration took place from December 2009, when she was more or less taken back to her basic structure before saloons were fitted, paint applied and deck and rails were fitted. Some six months later she was starting to take shape for her new role on Ullswater.

A tranquil scene at Glenridding in 2011. Both *Lady of the Lake* and *Raven* retain the ambience of their Victorian heritage, but also offer the facilities required by passengers in the twenty-first century, such as plenty of covered accommodation along with the provision of alcohol, hot drinks and snacks. Furthermore, passengers often like the option of special themed cruises such as jazz cruises, supper cruises as well as charter cruises for weddings, etc. Further heritage vessels have been added to the Ullswater fleet in recent years to compliment and to expand its work and profitability. *Lady Dorothy*, *Lady Wakefield* and *Western Belle* are able to offer more economic running and cater for times when passenger numbers are low. In addition, they allow a year-round service to cater for the ever-growing number of people that want to take a short break in the Lake District National Park.

4

Other Lakeland Steamers

The major centres for lake steamers in the Lake District have always been centred on Windermere and Ullswater. Despite this, other areas such as Derwent Water have always had lake steamers. Services also continue on Coniston and at the coast at Barrow-in-Furness, echoing the days of the Furness Railway.

Brochure advertising cruises on Derwent Water from around the 1950s. Motor launch cruises were offered from Keswick at two shillings and sixpence for the fifty-five-minute cruise. Self-drive motor boats were also offered from Keswick at ten shillings an hour and five launches were available for groups to hire. These were capable of carrying between 50 and 110 passengers.

Iris was owned by the well-known Lodore Swiss Hotel and was powered by a battery that was charged by the Lodore Falls behind the hotel. She was originally used to convey hotel guests around the lake. Edwardian guests of the Lodore Swiss Hotel are shown here embarking from the hotel's pier. (*J & C McCutcheon Collection*)

A traditional pleasure boat on Derwent Water showing Catbells around 1920. Cruises on Derwent Water give an exhilarating cruise on one of the most picturesque lakes. Breathtaking views of Skiddaw and other landmarks are gained on trips from places such as Lodore, Ashness Gate, High and Low Brandlehow and Hawes End. (*J & C McCutcheon Collection*)

The boat landing at Keswick around 1965. Launches leave Keswick for the fifty-minute cruise around the lake. Calls can be made at Ashness Gate, Lodore, High Brandlehow, Low Brandlehow, Hawes End and Nichol End. Derwent Water has never had the large steamers that are found elsewhere on lakes such as Windermere, Ullswater or Coniston, but retains a fine fleet of traditional varnished wooden-hull launches.

The epitome of Lake District steamer design – the *Gondola* cruising on Coniston in 2007. *Gondola* was built on the River Mersey by Jones Quiggin & Company. They were famous for the blockade runners that they constructed during the American Civil War. Steamer services by the LMS on Coniston survived until the Second World War, but weren't reintroduced after hostilities had ceased. The steamers were left to deteriorate and five years later in 1950, *Lady of the Lake* was scrapped. The *Gondola* found a new use as a houseboat in 1944, when she was sold to Mr Chanelor of Ulverston. During the early 1970s, a number of National Trust members campaigned for *Gondola* to be saved for the nation. The hull was floated once again, but was found to have deteriorated significantly. The restoration required a major fundraising campaign and eventually, *Gondola* was more or less rebuilt at Vickers Shipyard at Barrow-in-Furness. *Gondola* re-entered service in 1980 and today, after a long and varied career, she still operates as a graceful reminder of the Furness Railway and the days of the famed circular tour.

Gondola's saloons are most impressive and totally in keeping with her Victorian past. They are furnished with deep buttoned velvet upholstery with wood panelling and Corinthian columns decorated with enhancement in gold. They were painstakingly restored by the National Trust for *Gondola's* re-entry into service on Coniston.

If you look clearly, it is possible to see some reminders of the great age of Lakeland steamers. On the shores of Morecambe Bay, remnants of old piers can be seen. This image shows the once busy and now absent pier at Grange-over-Sands.

Gondola after being converted as a houseboat and lying half sunk and abandoned on Coniston in 1961 – twenty years later, she was restored by the National Trust. Derwent Water surprisingly never had a proper steamer service operating on it. The motor launches on Derwent Water are historic and most date back to Edwardian times before the First World War. Each take around 100 passengers and transport passengers in a world of beautifully varnished woodwork. The oldest are *May Queen* dating from 1904, *Iris* from 1908, and *Waterlily* from 1903.

Coniston now has two boats in regular service apart from the National Trust's *Gondola*. They are the *Ransome* and the *Ruskin*, and both date from the 1920s. These traditional looking steamers are powered by a twenty first-century power source as they were converted to solar-electric power in 2005.

Ruskin, on Coniston Water, is of traditional design and was built by the Chester Boat Company in 1922. When built, she was called *Raglan II*. *Ruskin* was built of mahogany on an oak frame. She's 40 feet in length with a width of 9 feet 6 inches and a depth of 3 feet. Initially, she gave cruises at Chester on the Dee. She saw service during the Second World War as a minesweeper (HMS *Ariel*) off the Dee Estuary and later saw use for air and sea rescue. She was purchased for further service on Coniston in 1992 and was renamed *Ruskin*.

Ramsome was named after one of the greatest writers on the Lake District – Arthur Ransome. She has a length of 40 feet, with a width of 11 feet 3 inches and a depth of 2 feet 9 inches. She was built of pitch pine on oak. *Ransome* was built as a small pleasure boat at Portsmouth and later saw service during the Second World War for the Admiralty, initially at Portsmouth and then later on the south coast and the River Thames. When de-requisitioned by the Admiralty at the end of the war, she was refitted and then operated by French Brothers at Windsor until the 1970s. She then saw service at Shepperton and underwent several name changes including *The Empress* and *Monarch I*. She was purchased for service on Coniston Water in 1994 and was renamed *Ransome*.

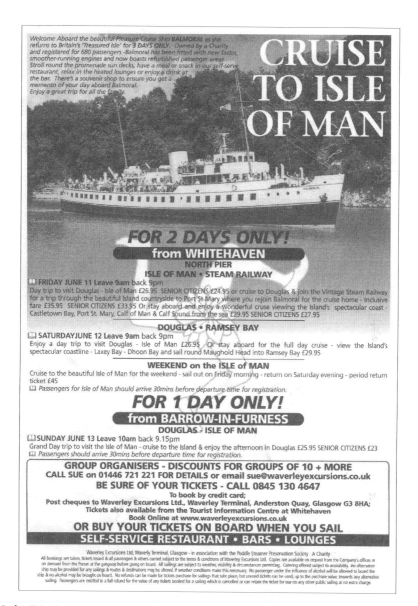

The Lake District was once served by a large number of coastal steamers. Apart from the Furness Railway, other steamer services included those across the Solway Firth to Annan and Dumfries as well as coastal services to the Isle of Man, Scotland and Liverpool. Most of these had short lives and are now rarely remembered. They failed due to a number of circumstances including the coming of the railways, silting of channels and the development of newer technology.

The only reminder of the great days of the large passenger pleasure steamer is the annual visits of the famous pleasure steamer *Balmoral* from places such as Barrow-in-Furness and Whitehaven. In the past, cruises have been offered along the Cumbrian coast to St Bees Head as well as to Blackpool, Morecambe and Fleetwood. The pleasure steamer *Balmoral* is now the only large passenger ship to offer cruises off the Cumbrian coast. She recreates, in some small way, the once common sight of conveying passengers by sea around the coast. The increasing deterioration of coastal piers now makes coastal steamer cruises harder to operate.

The story of Lake District steamers has come full circle. The past one hundred and fifty years has witnessed the building of a fine and purpose-built fleet of steamers to admire the scenic beauties of the English Lake District. The service has survived because of the wonderful craft that were designed by Victorian entrepreneurs. They designed craft that would impress the tripper and would provide a great level of luxury. Ultimately, they have provided the very best way to admire the changing seasonal landscapes. They have also changed very little over more than a century and provide the modern car-based visitor with the chance to leave the traffic jams behind and to view the Lake District National Park from the most perfect and most nostalgic of Lakeland inventions – the lake steamer. *Gondola* may have had her ups and downs, but today it gives the visitor of the twenty-first century the opportunity to sample what delighted those first Victorian visitors over 150 years ago!